English Country Gardens

English Country Gardens

Ethne Clarke & Clay Perry

Weidenfeld & Nicolson
London

First published in 1985 by
George Weidenfeld & Nicolson Ltd
91 Clapham High Street, London SW4 7TA

Designed by Simon Bell

ISBN 0 297 78507 9

Colour separations by Newsele Litho Ltd
Filmset by Keyspools Ltd, Golborne, Lancashire
Printed and bound in Italy by L.E.G.O. Vicenza

HALF TITLE PAGE Broadwell, Oxfordshire
TITLE PAGE Shamley Green, Surrey
OVERLEAF Shamley Green, Surrey

Acknowledgments

We would like to dedicate this book to the following people whose gardens are featured, and to thank them for their kind cooperation: Mr & Mrs J.V.Archer, Mr & Mrs Basil Baker, Mr & Mrs G.W.Barnes, Mrs Betts of Bladon Cottage, Mr & Mrs J.U.Body, Mr & Mrs W.Briault, Dr & Mrs M.Burton, Mr & Mrs Chambers of the The Belks, Mrs Grace Chandler, Mr & Mrs Chinnery of The Old Manor, Brig. & Mrs Cox, Mr & Mrs J.Darwin, Mr Dunn of Cerne Abbas, Mr & Mrs Farrier of Maple Tree House, Mr & Mrs A.Foot, Mr & Mrs R.W.S.Foulser, Mrs Fox of Trewardreva Farm, Mrs Molly Foster, Miss Graham of Thatch Cottage, Mr & Mrs C.Grey-Wilson, Caroline Hemming, Mr Hunt of Meadowside, Mr & Mrs J.J.Kinnear, Mrs Lane of Manor Cottage, John and Roger Last, Mrs Enid Makins, Mr & Mrs Marchant of The Old School House, Mrs Sherry Miller, Mr & Mrs D.Morris, Mr & Mrs H.Neale, The Lord Northbourne, Mr & Mrs Pemberton of The Quarter House, Mrs N.Phillips, Dr & Mrs Pratt of Field House, Mr & Mrs Raven of Lime Cottage, Mrs Audrey Richard, Mrs Ridley-Day of Sibton Park, The Hon. Mrs I.Rose, Maj. & Mrs W.Scott, Mr & Mrs D.Simmons, Mrs Sitwell of Apple Tree Cottage, Mr & Mrs K.Smedley, Mrs Smyth of Terra Cotta, Mr & Mrs J.Stevens, Mr & Mrs N.A.Stevens, Mrs Wendy Summers, Miss Tanner of The Wickets, Mr A.J.Thomas, Col. & Mrs Thorpe of Elm Cottage, Mr & Mrs H.Tricker, Mr Jack Tuck, Mr & Mrs A.Vousden, Mrs Wigram of Hidcote Boyce.

Special thanks are also due to Mr & Mrs R.Schofield, Mr & Mrs J.Kempston, Mrs Audrey Brereton, Mr & Mrs P.Williams, Mr & Mrs K.Broadbent, Mr & Mrs P.Morter, Maggie Perry, Donald & David Clarke, Mrs T.M.Reuss, and to the Rev. & Mrs Mumford of Cerne Abbas – 'It is the Blessing of the Almighty Husbandman, which imparts Success to such Labours of Love.'

Note on the captions: The village name and county precede each separate garden

Contents

Introduction

This book is an excursion through the glories of England's summer gardens, from small cottage plots, where old-fashioned flowers live in clever harmony with vegetables and fruit, to the more spacious gardens of manor house and rectory, where collections of choice plants are carefully sited to reveal a gardener's personal vision of Eden.

What gives an English garden its character? Certainly the climate is unique, for it is temperate, there are no prolonged extremes of heat and cold, the air is soft and the soil moist and fertile. The natural landscape is important, as are the materials from which dwellings and boundary walls are built, composing a pleasing setting. But these physical characteristics only contribute parts to the whole.

The key must be the English character. For if one's home is one's castle, the garden is an extension of it; historically, the English have treated the garden as a place deserving care and attention. Early in the last century, the American writer Washington Irving wrote in *Rural Life in England* that 'The taste of the English in the cultivation of land, and in what is called landscape-gardening, is unrivalled ... but what most delights me is the creative talent with which the English decorate the unostentatious abodes of middle life. ... The cherishing and training of some trees, the nice distribution of flowers and plants of tender and graceful foliage: all these are managed with a delicate tact, like the magic touching with which a painter finishes up a favourite picture.'

Gardening is an absorbing pastime, and those who fully succumb to it will devote all the time and care they can find, and then share the rewards of their enterprise. The friendly fraternity of gardeners is one of the oldest: 'God Almighty first planted a garden, and indeed it is the purest of human pleasures. ...' Walk along a village street or country lane, pause to admire the display of flowers and shrubs clustered around the front door, or peer over a wall wreathed in 'Albertine' roses, and the scene's creator will almost certainly appear, for gardeners are never far from their flowers.

There are few things of more interest to a gardener than another's garden, for it is through the interchange of ideas, old and new, that gardeners learn from each other and draw inspiration from the gardens they visit. Once inside the gate, we can compare plants and plantings, uncover the history of the land and examine the qualities that have given the place its special character.

In the eighteenth century, William Shenstone wrote that gardening could be divided into three types: landscape, parterre and kitchen, and gardeners divided into three sorts accordingly. Having spent an entire summer travelling through southern England, meeting more than a hundred gardeners and viewing their creations, I arrived at a similar conclusion, only changing the names of the categories: there are those for whom the design of the garden is all important, and who put the plants to work within the scheme; others whose main interest is collecting, to make a garden including, for example, only plants and herbs grown in gardens before the eighteenth century, or simply as many kinds of pinks as possible. Then there are the 'mad enthusiasts', and I give them that appellation with special affection: they will try to grow anything they get their hands on, 'just to see what sprouts', and they can turn any space into a garden.

Three hundred years ago, John Worlidge wrote '. . . there is scarcely a cottage in most of the southern parts of England but hath its proportionable gardens . . .', and a tour today around these counties reveals this still to be the case.

However, this is not meant to imply that gardens in the other parts of England, and Great Britain for that matter, are not just as absorbing. I regret that time and space have not allowed us to follow the trail of gardening tradition from Land's End to John o'Groats! I longed particularly to visit the gardens of the Malvern region, for example, for it was there that my own love affair with this subject began as a child, twenty-five years ago, in the garden of my aunt's Victorian villa.

In my aunt's garden there were many rooms: in the glasshouse of the kitchen garden the night-blooming cactus flowered, to everyone's wonder; rose beds bordered the green tennis lawn, and provided magnificently perfumed blooms for me to gather by the basketful; and in the flower garden the delphiniums and

foxgloves, pinks and pansies grew in borders of such luxuriant colour and scent that I dreamt myself transported to some storybook paradise. My discovery of this place must have been decreed by fate, for the rest of my childhood was spent in midwestern America, where you can hear the corn grow, but where roses and herbaceous flowers have a tenuous hold on existence.

To follow the season from Cornwall to Norfolk must surely be one of the greatest pleasures for any garden lover. Beginning in the Cotswolds during early summer, the fading blossoms of spring-flowering bulbs are replaced by cheerful violas, and by the blowsy beauty of the peony; there is a striking contrast with the Mediterranean exuberance of warm Cornish gardens, already ablaze with colour.

Midsummer finds the gardens of Norfolk swooning under their headily scented mantle of old shrub roses, or engulfed in stands of azure delphiniums; Dorset and Somerset gardens drowse amid the buzz of bees, working sweetly scented herbs against a background of golden thatch. The season progresses along the floral borders of Suffolk, which provide a feast of colour and perfume, and draws to its close as Kent and Sussex pull on their cloak of soft autumn shades.

The book is arranged in three sections, dividing the weeks of summer into a gardener's chronicle. The introductory text of each section serves as a diary, recording observations from prevailing weather conditions, events in the garden at this or that part of the season, and other subjects of immediate concern, to the writings of the earliest gardening authors, on flowers and plantings, garden ornament and design, festivals and bees: all inspired by the gardeners I met and the wonderful diversity of gardens they have created.

BROADWELL
OXFORDSHIRE

Early Summer

Now it is June and ... the honey Dews sweeten the Ayr and the Sunny Showers are the comfort of the Earth; ... the azure Sky showes the Heavens are gracious, and the glorious Sun glads the spirit of Nature ... I hold it a sweet season, the Senses perfume and the Spirits comfort.

The Twelve Moneths, M.Stevenson, 1661

There is a distinct air of freshness in all parts of the garden during June, as roses, irises, magnolias and many other flowers of soft hue and sweet fragrance replace the dried and fading leaves of spring-flowering bulbs and shrubs.

The character of this month is disclosed by the garden's demeanour; and in June, Flora is demure and a little coy. One has heard of 'shrinking violets', and the phrase is well turned when you consider how reticent are the blossoms of *Viola odora*, hiding among clusters of heart-shaped leaves in the shadier recesses of the garden. Yet how unlike their cousins are the violas and pansies that clown about in June flower beds! Varieties available today are descendants of the old-fashioned 'Heartsease', *V. tricolor*, that carries the colours of early summer, with thumbnail-sized flowers in tints of blue and pale mauve, yellow the colour of rich cream, and white.

For many years, pansies were cherished as Florist's flowers, cultivated and improved by that group whose goal was the creation through selective breeding of perfectly shaped and coloured flowers. Tradition has it that in 1813, a certain Lord Gambier set his gardener to work raising seedlings of a form of *V. tricolor* his lordship had gathered in the woods. The gardener soon noticed that the flowers were much improved by the attention lavished on them. But even then this was not a new discovery, for in 1629, John Parkinson wrote that 'These plants were first wilde, and by manuring brought to be both fairer in colour, and peradventure of a better sent then when they grew wilde.'

Large-flowered pansies are common in windowbox and border, but they are sometimes so outsize that the flowers can't hold their heads up! Violas have better posture, and offer great potential for eye-catching colour; for example, 'Irish Molly' is an unusual greenish-purple that associates well with the green-flowered auriculas and grey-green hostas.

One of the greatest pleasures of June is the flowering of the old-fashioned shrub roses. For many of them, this is the only time of year they bloom, so we must take time to enjoy the infinite beauty of the flowers, in colours shading from pearly white to dark claret red, with silk and velvet-textured petals and a perfume unequalled by any other member of the floral kingdom. The raspberry-scented Bourbon roses, with cup-shaped flowers, have old-world charm and the attribute of flowering for most of the summer; the variety 'Madame Isaac Periere' possesses what is probably the most powerful rose perfume, given off by enormous flat, double magenta flowers. It makes a large bush of arching branches that will, given a rich deeply dug soil, carry a profusion of blooms into September.

Increasing hours of sunshine, clear blue skies and warm westerly winds keep the gardener busy this month with watering, for although there may be sudden heavy thunderstorms, they tend to be brief and water does not actually penetrate the soil enough to have any lasting benefit. Thus June is often the driest month.

Watering is best done in the early evening or late afternoon, when the sun is low in the sky, so that the water does not evaporate immediately, and has a chance to penetrate to the plant roots. And care must be taken to ensure that enough water is given. However tedious it may be lugging a watering can from tap to plant, and tempting to decide 'one will do', persevere. Watering that wets only the surface soil will draw the plant roots upwards, exposing them to danger and even causing early death.

Mulching has a leading role in the gardener's repertoire. The laying down of a blanket of half-decomposed organic matter between plants goes a long way to conserving moisture in the soil, and has the advantage of helping to check weed growth. And the flowers look particularly lovely seen against the background of a dark mulch, rather like showing precious jewels on a velvet cushion.

To be effective, a mulch must be at least two inches thick, and kept in place and renewed as the scratching of birds and the natural action of weather and worms takes it into the soil. And it is essential that the soil is deeply moist and cool (not cold) before the mulch is put in place. That may seem strange, but for as much as a mulch keeps moisture in, it also keeps it out. Plants benefit more from even and constant moisture than from alternate periods of drought and drenching, and enjoy the steady coolness of the soil rather than soil that is baked by day and chilled by night.

Peat moss is a popular mulch, dark and luxuriant, and will also improve the texture of the soil as it is taken in, as will other organic mulches. Cocoa hulls, nut shells, and woodbark (specially treated to remove detrimental resins) have the same dark attractiveness, but are rather more conspicuous and certainly more robust than peat, so are better suited to mulching shrubs than violets. Straw, grass clippings (partially dried before use), seaweed, pine needles and plastic sheeting are all good mulch material. But since plastic holds the warmth of the soil, it should be used chiefly around heat-loving plants; tomatoes grown through plastic are less prone to blossom end rot and greenback because of the constant even moisture; they make rapid growth and ripen faster.

Garden visiting is one of the delights of an English summer. Often, whole villages throw open their gardens and provide the visitor with an opportunity to savour the unique character of the community. And as one moves from manor house to vicarage to cottage, sampling the delights of each garden, one becomes aware, through the recurring use of certain distinctive plants or of similar schemes, of the gardener's network: an informal, but immensely important organization devoted to the swapping of cuttings, exchange of ideas and experiences, and the offering of unsolicited advice – favourite gardening pastimes.

The designing of a garden is a highly personal, if not emotional, subject. Over the centuries, as many volumes have been written as there have been years, purporting to describe exactly how a garden should be made.

To many, the cottage garden is the ideal, and often serves as a model when a new garden is being planned, particularly in these stressful times when we yearn to recapture the past in an attempt to reassure ourselves. But as the image of a cottage garden varies from person to person, so their interpretations differ distinctly. Some would hold that a cottage garden must consist of vegetables and fruit grown in beds on either side of a straight path leading to the front door, with flowers and shrubs mixed in artless merriment around the outer perimeters of the property. Others scoff at this, and decree that shady walks, winding through beds in which flowers, vegetables and shrubs are randomly mixed, are the sign of a true cottage garden.

Yet there are qualities shared by the numerous cottage-style gardens all over England: chiefly an unconscious elegance and lack of artifice that can only be achieved by someone whose chief purpose and pleasure is to grow simple flowers and vegetables, in a manner entirely unaffected and in harmony with Nature. And usually all the plants required can be had from seed and cuttings the gardener has gathered and rooted himself – as cottage gardeners are a thrifty lot.

They are also natural garden designers, relying on some inborn sense of what is appropriate, rather than on any skills acquired through professional training. William Robinson wrote in *The English Flower Garden*: 'Among the things made by man nothing is prettier than an English cottage garden, and they often teach lessons that "great" gardeners should learn . . . .'

The flowers most often encountered in a cottage garden are uncomplicated: pinks, hollyhocks, delphiniums, sunflowers, irises, lilies, roses and honeysuckle to name but a few. You may discover the odd exotica, grown for the pleasure of a challenge, but it is the old varieties of hardy perennials, tried and true, that are the substance of the garden. These plants became established as cottage-garden flowers because they are able to fend for themselves, requiring little attention, as the cottager hadn't the time or the facility to coddle tender varieties.

Many of the plants would have been familiar in gardens 500 years ago, and have histories as delightful as their perfume: for scent was a quality cottagers valued in their flowers, as well as the practical uses to which the plant could be put, since the garden had to provide for the physical as well as the spiritual well-being of the family. Plants were included to feed the bees who made the honey and pollinated the orchard; from the petals fragrant oils were extracted to flavour sauces or sweeten the air; herb branches were gathered to use for seasoning, freshen cupboards and cure simple ailments.

A cottage garden is above all things a place of uncontrived beauty, easily enjoyed, where labour is well-rewarded and quiet pleasures satisfied. In 1568, Thomas Hyll wrote in *The Proffitable Arte of Gardening*: 'The Garden is made perfect, delectable, and profitable ... and wee then receive by it two speciall commodities. The first is profit, which riseth through the encrease of Hearbs and flowers: the other is pleasure, verie delectable through the delight of walking in the same ...', and went on to remind us that the fresh air of the garden imbued with the sweet smell of flowers bestowed health and well-being.

LECHLADE
GLOUCESTERSHIRE

In June the colour and shape of foliage is often more striking than that of the flowers. This can be used to good effect, so that a planting is of interest even before the flowers bloom. Many waterside plants have attractive greenery. Here the broad flat leaves of arum lilies contrast with the feathery fronds of astilbe, and round-leaved caltha plays off the slender blades of iris – an impressive complement to the tiny flowers of arabis and candelabra primulas.

A low arch clipped in the tight hedge on the far side of this garden was an invitation to stroll through it and across the close-cut lawn to discover what lay beyond: on this side, a sweep of well-ordered terrace bisected by a flower-edged path, and at the edge a quiet glade surrounding a lily pond. On the other side of the hedge are herbaceous beds separated from it by another expanse of lawn, so that the green spaces serve to divide the garden into rooms. The open spaces and the individual characters of each planting area make the garden seem larger than it really is.

A still sheet of water reflects the overhanging magnolia branches and drooping sprays of hellebore, muting the already tender colours of these flowering plants; the simple shape and uncluttered edge of the tiny pond are echoed by the simplicity of the surrounding planting. Water in a garden alters the dimensions of the place: a pond makes the sky a part of the ground beneath our feet, giving the garden a quiet focus, while a babbling brook makes music and movement.

Broadwell
OXFORDSHIRE

Euphorbia characias and its subspecies *wulfenii* are everywhere about in the early summer border, and were recommended by Gertrude Jekyll because there are few other 'large growing plants with good foliage' at this time of year. Peonies, on the other hand, provide good clumps of leaves with the bonus of stunning flowers. The old-fashioned crimson-red *Paeonia officinalis* when joined in a simple association with the acid-drop-yellow polka dots of the euphorbia bracts, makes an especially fine composition of subtle contrasts of colour and shape.

A pretty centrepiece for the forecourt of a garden is made from a beautifully carved Italian trough. Such a dramatic ornament should be given a commanding position, and accompanying planting kept in a relatively low key. Around the pedestal grey-leaved lamb's ears and the tiny white flowers of cerastium contrast with the glossy evergreen dwarf box edging, and the grey-green scheme is repeated in the trough with *Hebe pinguifolia* and variegated thyme. Thus the display attracts the eye without offending.

The flower border in early summer is best used to provide 'incidents of good bloom' and colour, since many of the finest herbaceous plants perform later in the season. In this length of border the eye travels from clumps of red peony to deep purple aquilegia bells, pausing along the way to rest on the soft greys of phlomis and yellow spikes of *Heuchera cylindrica* that spill on to the pebble path. But the contrasting shapes of leaf and habit give movement and unity to this border, long before the full flush of flowers occurs.

KENCOT
OXFORDSHIRE

One of the most gratifying pleasures of gardening is in the raising of plants from seeds and cuttings. As Leonard Mascall wrote in 1572: 'yea nothing more discovereth onto us the great and incomprehensible worke of God, that of one little Pepin sede, Nut or small plant, may come to the selfsame herb or tree and to bring forth infinite of the same fruit . . . .' Trays of seedlings and cuttings can be found in almost every garden, growing on until they are of a size to be planted out or potted up and sold at church bazaars or given to friends. They are evidence of the gardener's skill, patience and thrift.

The front garden is rather like the cover of a book, illustrating the contents of the garden behind the house, or announcing the likelihood of rewards for looking closer. But unlike some book covers, the front garden is usually an accurate indicator of the nature of the main garden. The abundant planting in front of this Cotswold cottage, spilling out on to the street in a frill of aubretia, saxifrage and violas, with clumps of honeysuckle dressing the old village pump, prepares you for the astonishing variety of horticultural activity that goes on in the small garden behind the cottage. A square of lawn and vegetable garden is flanked by two greenhouses, a sizeable coldframe, mist propagator, espaliered pear tree, a small bed of plant treasures, and a collection of bonsai raised from seed – of course!

KENCOT
OXFORDSHIRE

Roses and wisteria are a
beautiful sight when grown
together, as they frequently
are. But once the mauve-
coloured wisteria has finished
blooming, it is as well to have
another climber in flower to
sustain interest. Preferably,
this should be a plant that will
begin flowering before the
wisteria fades, and carry on for
a long period. *Abutilon
vitifolium* answers these
requirements, though is not
widely grown, probably
because of its reputation for
tenderness. But given a warm
wall, abutilon is fast-growing,
up to ten feet, and has
attractive vine-shaped grey-
green leaves and delicate
white or mauve hollyhock-like
flowers. The hybrid
A. × suntense has larger
flowers in white and shades of
blue and purple.

BURFORD
OXFORDSHIRE

Tucked into a sun-filled south-
facing corner on the banks of
the river Windrush, lies a
cheerful small garden where
the sound of rushing water
blankets the noise of the
nearby busy bridge. Wisely,
the planting of the retaining
walls has been kept simple,
with hummocks of familiar
aubretia and saxifrage giving
way to red, pink and yellow
helianthemums; the remainder
of the garden, constantly moist
and beautifully warm, is
devoted to the cultivation of
choicer plants.

Churchill
OXFORDSHIRE

Breathtaking effects in a garden are not necessarily achieved through exhausting effort and complicated plantings; the simple approach frequently meets with the greatest success. The entrance to this village garden could hardly be more enticing, with masses of *Clematis montana*, like a floral Milky Way, underplanted with irises in variety to continue the display after the clematis is past (for its brief flowering period is its only serious fault).

It takes a certain amount of courage to give a rampant climber like *Clematis montana* such free rein, and to make such a strong use of a single species, but the effect of draping a simple cottage with garlands of starry flowers raises it from the ordinary to the unique. On a building more ornate, this treatment would be quite wrong, disguising the architectural value rather than enhancing it.

Few sights are more gratifying to the gardener's eye than rows of young vegetables set out against a dark, well-tilled soil. Lines of broad beans, early peas and cabbages and the first runner beans breaking through the soil are the gardener's blue chip investments, for the kitchen garden pays dividends in pleasure as well as profit. But to be successful, the gardener must lavish as much care on the vegetables as on the choice plants in the flower garden.

The columbine, *Aquilegia vulgaris*, is, in the words of Shirley Hibberd from his volume *Familiar Garden Flowers*, 'an old-fashioned garden flower that everybody knows and loves, and yet very few make it the subject of any special care in cultivation'. Chaucer mentioned it, as did Shakespeare; the herbalist John Parkinson thought that a decoction made from the seeds aided childbirth. Columbines are hardy perennials that like sun or light shade. They are short-lived, but seed themselves freely; young plants pop up in the most unexpected places. There are many species and hybrids to choose from, with flowers either single and long-spurred or double and spurless, ranging in colour from white, shades of red and yellow to 'stone-blue, or deep night-brown'.

HIDCOTE BOYCE
GLOUCESTERSHIRE

There are garden pictures that owe their beauty not to any conscious effort on the part of the gardener, but simply to the natural grace of the plants themselves, growing in easy associations. Here a wall of honey-coloured Cotswold stone supports a cascade of ivy crowned with ruby-red peony; pale lilacs and mauve irises begin their gentle fade to be followed by roses and lavender. There are times when it is as well to leave plants to their own devices, helping them only by judicious thinning to avoid an overgrown and untended appearance.

The *laissez-faire* approach to gardening is well suited to public-spirited gardeners, who will use their skills to beautify each part of their village, from lamp-post to post-box, using plants that require little attention to give of their best. Among the finest for this purpose are the many species of cotoneaster; they will grow anywhere as long as the soil is well drained, and look best if left unpruned. There are several species that make attractive evergreen fans against walls, bearing flowers in early summer followed by glowing red berries. *C. conspicuus* 'Decorus' and *C. microphyllus* are both reliably evergreen; *C. horizontalis*, the 'herringbone' cotoneaster, is the old cottage garden familiar, but *C. apiculatus* has larger fruit and finer foliage.

CONSTANTINE
CORNWALL

Hidden behind a lattice-windowed door, sheltered by high yew hedges, lies a place that has more than a touch of *The Secret Garden* about it, the image heightened by the excitement of the gardener's granddaughter, who chattered about the beauty of 'my grannie's flowers'. Paths edged with lines of close-clipped box border beds of pinks and old roses, creating the sort of small enclosed spaces originally designed to complement the early eighteenth-century house, providing all the flowers needed indoors. All too often the design and purpose of an old garden are lost over the generations. Then a note of sadness creeps in as a charming example of English gardening tradition becomes just another vegetable patch.

What pleasure it gives to find scented plants gathered round the garden gate, so that entrances and exits are accomplished with accompanying drifts of floral fragrance. The velvety grey-green leaves of *Geranium macrorrhizum* have a spicy perfume that mingles well with the sharp citrus smell of variegated mint. These plants are growing at the foot of a fine *Magnolia sieboldii*, with finely scented bowl-shaped flowers that have a curious habit, seeming to stare you straight in the eye.

WOODCOTE
GLOUCESTERSHIRE

The bright blue bells of muscari are gone and turning to seed, but this cottage garden path retains its vitality with a simple scheme of wallflowers and primulas, cerastium and aubretia. Paths and planting should always be related to the style of the cottage entrance – in this case, austerely simple lines of window and door are repeated by the straightness of the path, but the short dogleg at the threshold relieves any feeling of monotony and makes the necessary end to path and flower edging.

CADGWITH COVE
CORNWALL

Eschscholzia, the Californian poppy; *Gladiolus byzantinus*, a dainty wine-red gladiolus that grows wild on the sun-baked island of Crete; golden pot marigolds and crimson roses: all dancing against the shining white and blue cottage – this vibrant play of colour is typical of many Cornish gardens, where it dispels memories of cold winter winds off the Atlantic. There is a lesson here for gardeners everywhere: a mass of flowers predominantly of one shade will directly influence mood. Gertrude Jekyll wrote of gold gardens that to enter one 'even on the dullest day, will be like coming into sunshine'.

CADGWITH COVE
CORNWALL

Here a herbaceous border nestles below a winding footpath opposite an ancient alehouse, once the den of smugglers. A steep lane leads into the village, hidden from view and lying hard against the sea. The welcome surprise of finding soft grey thatch (where everything else has been granite and slate) is intensified by the sudden burst of flower colour and scent. Woodbine clings to the side wall, and a fuchsia hedge begins to lend its nodding crimson blossoms, while in the border opposite, fringe-petalled oriental poppies spring up behind a cushion of cranesbill, and a furry grey mullein soars skyward. There is a purple-flowered species, *Verbascum phoeniceum*, that recalls the tradition that Phoenician merchantmen traded with the Cornish tin miners.

BURYAS BRIDGE
CORNWALL

The creeks and river valleys of the Cornish south coast shelter some startling gardens in their leafy glades, where 'the earth/ Made pregnant by the streams gave birth/ To thymy herbage and gay flowers,/ And when drear winter frowns and lowers/ In spots less genial, ever here/ Things bud and burgeon through the year.' In this southerly latitude, the combination of warm breezes, plenty of sunshine, and well-drained soil stimulates the verdant growth of plants, so that the ardent gardener can, in the relatively short space of a year, create a garden that appears to have been tended for much longer.

Making a new garden from a grassy field is a challenge to be dealt with either in slow measured paces or met head-on, as this gardener chose to do. Over twelve months of unstinting effort, with plants raised from seed and cuttings, she transformed a field into series of small beds lined by rambling paths that lead through the flowerbeds to a vantage point of a sunny raised terrace near the house. From there, surrounded with fragrant herbs, one looks down towards the stream and the tall-growing lilac and elder that border the property. A terrace is a fine feature for a garden of whatever size, as John James noted in *The Theory and Practice of Gardening* (1712): 'from the height of one terrace all the lower parts of the garden may be discovered . . . and presents us with very agreeable views.'

The dappled shade of overhanging trees, the well-drained loose soil and the freedom to colonize by self-sown seedlings encourage a brilliant display of foxgloves. *Digitalis purpurea*, the common purple foxglove, is native to the British Isles where it grows freely in hedgerows throughout early summer. It and the yellow-flowered *D. grandiflora syn. ambigua* were popular in cottage gardens as long ago as the early 1500s, and Parkinson remarks that some called them finger-flowers, 'because they are like unto the fingers of a glove, the ends cut off'. Foxgloves are hardy biennials; seed planted in early summer will be ready for planting out by September. In the border the hybrid 'Excelsior' strain makes the best show, with exceedingly tall, densely crowded flower spikes.

The amount of time spent nurturing plants is a measure of a gardener's devotion, as is the affection in which the plants are held. Many gardeners find when moving to a new home that it is as necessary to bring along cherished plants as to transport the furniture, for it cheers the heart to see a familiar face in a strange setting, and relieves the 'just-planted' appearance of a new garden. Every square inch of this small Cornish garden is planted with such old friends and favourite flowers, and one could not turn without encountering some pretty composition of flower and leaf.

NANCENOYE
CORNWALL

In his book *The Old Shrub Roses*, Graham Stuart Thomas remarks that he came upon a bush of 'Fantin-Latour' growing in a garden, and simply labelled 'Best Garden Rose'. This is surely one of the finest old-fashioned roses, and if one had space for only a single bush, or were starting a garden devoted to old roses, 'Fantin-Latour' would be an excellent first choice. It blooms only once in early summer, but it has a neat rounded habit, and a healthy bush will be smothered in deliciously fragrant, shell-pink flowers.

CONSTANTINE
CORNWALL

'No annual is better for a warm bank or any place with full sunny exposure', wrote Gertrude Jekyll about *Eschscholzia*, the Californian poppy, a true sun-worshipper that snaps its petals firmly shut as evening draws in. Miss Jekyll could have added that few annuals flower over such a long period, or sow themselves as prodigiously. The Spaniards first encountered it in the New World, and the flowers so thickly blanketed the terrain that the region was referred to as the 'Land of Fire'. In 1833 it was introduced to England, and later became the flower emblem of its native California. So it was highly appropriate to find it shining out in every corner of a garden belonging to an American expatriate, who is herself a transplant from the 'Land of Fire'.

Cracks and crevices in low-rising granite steps leading to a long terrace make an ideal home for china-blue *Convolvulus mauritanicus*, and the dwarf erigeron, with its tiny pink and white daisy flowers. Luckily, the convolvulus does not have the invasive habit of its relation the bindweed; but neither is it as hardy, so in cool climates it appreciates a warm, well-drained spot. In contrast, dwarf erigeron is an easy plant, revelling in gritty soil and self-sowing into almost any nook or cranny. Small carpeting plants such as this should be used to link walls and steps with the main body of the garden.

47

FREMINGTON
DEVONSHIRE

There are two approaches to
this garden: the main one
takes you through a wooden
door where a poem is posted,
cautioning you to slow your
pace and tune your senses to
the sound of quiet; the second,
though not intended as the
entrance, beckons with a rose-
covered arch. It brings you
into a part of the garden that is
bursting with colour, scent
and bee-song, which rushes up
to greet you as you enter.
Beds of standard roses
are discovered, lavishly
underplanted with clove-
scented pinks, bright-faced
pansies, islands of thyme and
an ocean of self-sown regal
lilies, making ready to add
their grace and perfume to a
floral phantasmagoria.

In just under fifteen years, the
gardening partnership of
husband and wife have
brought into being their dream
of a cottage garden. Created
from a dull field that was once
part of a country estate, the
only remaining parts of which
are the fine brick walls and
elegant gazebo dating from
1747, the garden is divided into
areas, each possessed of its
own distinct character. Yet the
leitmotif of the garden unites
each zone, established both by
the innumerable varieties of
old-fashioned roses that are
planted throughout, and by the
consistent use of plants typical
of a cottage garden.

The open ball-shaped flowerhead of *Allium christophii* appears to be made of tiny lavender stars, and like the other species in the flowering onion tribe (including garlic, onions and chives), makes an eye-catching show in the flower garden. All the species carry their flower umbels at the top of straight, sturdy stems rising from a cluster of strap-like leaves that smell of onions when bruised. *A. moly*, the Golden Garlic, was credited by Homer to have saved Ulysses from being turned into a pig, and has over the centuries been valued as an ingredient for magic potions. Moly has pretty yellow flowers and grows to about ten inches; *A. christophii* can reach two feet, but the tallest is the purple-flowered *A. giganteum* with tight flower clusters five inches across atop four-foot tall stems. All the alliums bloom in early summer, and most appreciate an open sunny position in light soil.

Mrs Earle wrote, in *Pot Pourri from a Surrey Garden*, 'A good deal of real gardening pleasure and satisfactory ornamental effect is to be had from growing plants in pots and tubs, vases and vessels of all kinds, both in small and big gardens.' The chief 'gardening pleasure' is had from enlarging the available growing space, and thereby the number of plants that can be grown – a persistent desire of any keen gardener. The ornamental effect is obvious; an arid wasteland of paved patio or forecourt can be transformed into a welcoming extension of the main garden. The picture is completed by dressing the background walls with climbing roses, wisteria, clematis and cotoneaster, which can also be cultivated in pots and tubs if there is no access to the earth.

Shamley Green
SURREY

Postcard perfect, this Surrey farmhouse and its overflowing flower garden rest peacefully at the foot of hillside pasture. Behind the delphinium screen are rows and beds of peas and pansies, cabbages and calendulas, dianthus and dahlias. Beyond the flowerbeds are the beehives, fruit trees and small glasshouses in which the gardener preserves treasures such as trumpet-flowered datura. Her efforts, and those of her children and grandchildren, are watched and commented upon by an old green parrot perched in an apple tree.

The Queen of the flowers and the one most favoured in English gardens, the rose is 'loved by all grades and ages, from the little village child who wreather it from the hedgerow in his sister's hair, to the princess who holds it in her gemmed *bouquetier*, so it may be alike enjoyed in the labourer's garden or in the conservatory of the peer'. But perhaps nowhere does the rose seem more at home than in the country garden where, grown from cuttings pushed into the soil, it sends up its branches to crown the garden with fragrant, soft-petalled blooms.

SHAMLEY GREEN
SURREY

Facing on to the village green, the front garden of this cottage is framed by a rose arch, the warm colour of the flowers echoing the warmth of the brickwork. In her volume *Roses*, Gertrude Jekyll remarked that people should look around their properties for aspects that would be 'made beautiful by the use of free-growing Roses'. While much use is made of climbing plants to disguise that which is unsightly (which is what Miss Jekyll had in mind), they can also be used to transform an aspect that is merely unremarkable. Here training a rambling rose over a wire arch makes a simple white gate as elegant as one of fine wrought iron.

Seen against the tapestry of a herbaceous border, an island bed of roses and pansies introduces a note of Victorian formality, for it was then the fashion to grow roses in isolation from the rest of the garden in beds surrounded by gravel walks. This was the 'Rosarium', and as William Paul wrote in *The Rose Garden*, 'No one who really loves Roses will be content with viewing a plant placed in the back of a border. . . . To fully appreciate its beauties one must have it directly under the eye. . . .' Modern hybrid tea and floribunda roses do have more effect when planted *en masse* rather than dotted individually around the pleasure garden; their growth is more restrained than old-fashioned shrub roses, so they are more likely to sink into anonymity among other flowers. They also require greater attention and pruning, and spraying becomes less of a chore if the plants can be treated as a group.

CRANLEIGH
SURREY

It is an unwritten law that as gardeners grow older their gardens seem to become larger and more demanding of attention, and unless one is able to drum up assistance to share the labour often only two options remain: to rip up the flowerbeds, plant trees, shrubs and groundcover, and reduce the lawn area with gravel or paving (extremely disconcerting to a real gardener), or to move to a smaller garden, where one can still have the pleasures of flowers and grassy sward, but on a more manageable scale. This garden is an example of the latter. Although not yet mature, it recaptures for the owners the variety and beauty of their previous and much larger garden.

By raising the border with a low stone retaining wall, the work of tending the plants it contains is made easier; small clumps of groundcovering plants begin their sprawl and in the end will reduce the amount of weeding necessary. A purple clematis shambles through an easy-growing white cluster rose, and none of the plants included in the scheme requires undue amounts of attention – except perhaps the reddish-bronze begonias lined up in front of the low grey wall. But it is the trademark of a garden lover always to make the effort to achieve the desired effect: not only do the begonias and stone create an attractive colour scheme, but the begonias soften the transition from lawn edge to raised bed.

CRANLEIGH
SURREY

The quiet colour harmony created by the cool creamy-white blooms of the rose 'Iceberg' floating above golden achillea is given a piquancy by the intermingled sprays of cardinal red lobelia. Gardening is a skill, like cooking or music, that entails combining individual parts to make a whole: it is necessary to avoid the use of wrong notes or incompatible flavours. Another useful comparison would be with painting, since form and colour are the most important considerations in both pursuits, and by using these elements in harmony or in contrast, we can create scenes that please or offend, soothe or startle.

Having moved from a garden that was becoming too large, this Surrey gardener set out to create a flower garden that was full of interest and colour for at least ten months of the year, making great use of plants with variegated or tinted foliage and a wide variety of species and hybrid clematis. The garden plan revolves around an old walnut tree, with vegetable garden, shrubbery, water garden and herbaceous border set out around the perimeter. The border is backed by a pergola covered with roses and clematis, so that one side of the garden is a wall of flowers.

From the terrace, where a fringe of low-growing foliage plants is the main interest, the eye travels in easy progression along the length of the border, from one small colour group to another; the undulations of warm colours that appear to advance and cool colours that recede enhance the sinuous line of the border, giving the garden an illusion of greater width.

From the opposite end of the border, looking back towards the house over a clump of golden variegated lemon balm, red-tinged *Fuchsia gracilis* 'Versicolor', clusters of pinks and lavender pansies, the picture brings to mind Gertrude Jekyll's observation that 'The first purpose of a garden is to give happiness and repose of mind, which is more often enjoyed in the contemplation of the homely border'.

This elegant little planting is an example of the effects to be had by successfully contrasting leaf colour, shape, and habit of growth. Canary yellow *Lysimachia nummularia* creeps over the grey paving stones at the edge of a small pond. The yellow tone is picked up by *Alchemilla mollis*, and by golden variegated thyme, which mingles its tiny purple flowers with the yellow ones of the lysimachia. The spiky green-and-white leaves of gardener's garters adds height, and makes a pleasing contrast both with the water lily leaves floating on the water, and the looser, rounded habit of the alchemilla.

LONGSTOCK
HAMPSHIRE

The romantic vision of English cottage gardens has been lovingly portrayed in the paintings of Helen Allingham: rosy-cheeked children gambol under an arbour of roses, while hollyhocks scrape the thatched eaves of a half-timbered cottage. Having once lived in a house pictured by Allingham, it became this gardener's obsession to recreate just such a garden, using plants that have been cherished in cottage gardens for centuries. The result is a small garden of great charm, where the relation of plants, garden design and house, is faithful to the easy grace and simple nature of the original.

ALBURY
SURREY

In 1577, Thomas Hyll wrote of the several virtues of walkways through a garden: 'the one is that the owner may diligently view the properitie of his herbes and flowers, the other for the delight and comfort of his wearied mind, which he may ... conceyve in the delectable sightes and fragrant smelles of the flowers, by walking up and down, and about the Garden in them. ...' This Surrey house and garden, built on the site of an Elizabethan manor of which only the dovecote remains, follows in its simple way Hyll's eloquent premise. To walk among the flowerbeds, plucking a fragrant nosegay of purple sage, lavender and feverfew, and to then look back at the house and its great chimneys, is to step back into one of the lost gardens of Renaissance England.

SHAMLEY GREEN
SURREY

Many of the flowers that are
traditionally the most common
in cottage gardens are those
that are hardy, free with their
flowers and require little
attention, because cottagers
were mostly preoccupied with
the daily struggle for
existence, and regarded their
energy better spent tending
vegetables. Many plants were
adopted from the surrounding
countryside, their qualities
improved by domestication.
But quite a few of the plants
introduced to England from
other parts of the world found
their way into humble gardens
from the altogether grander
ones of the gentry, which
frequently served as trial
grounds for newly discovered
species. How and when the
yellow-flowered loosestrife
(*Lysimachia punctata*) arrived
in English gardens is
uncertain, but so hardy is it
that it is now found as a
common weed in boggy places,
as well as in many borders. Not
surprisingly, it needs a firm
hand to keep it under control,
but the flowers do make a
bright show of brash yellow.

CRANLEIGH
SURREY

'Old Sally's was a long, low,
thatched cottage with
diamond-paned windows
winking under the eaves and a
rustic porch smothered in
honeysuckle. . . . Sally had
such flowers, and so many of
them . . . It seemed as though
all the roses in Lark Rise had
gathered together in that one
garden.' Cottages crumble and
their gardens fall under the
plough, just as varieties of
roses fall in and out of fashion
and favour, and vanish
from cultivation. So it is
encouraging to find a garden
where a particular variety, in
this case 'Prunella Poulsen', is
retained and cherished by the
gardener, to bring forth yearly
its wonderful display of
blushing pink flowers.

Easton
HAMPSHIRE

Lavender bushes bank the streetside of this cottage garden, mingling their sweet perfume with the spicy scent of the white-flowered *Dianthus* 'Mrs Sinkins', edging the curving path to the cottage door. She is just one of many clove-scented pinks (bred from *D. plumarius*) that, along with the old clove carnations, or gilliflower (bred from *D. caryophyllus*), rank with the rose and the lily as the most treasured of cottage-garden flowers. John Parkinson called the gilliflower the 'pride of our English gardens', and of all the varieties, the Old Crimson Clove was most valued: Gerard wrote that a conserve made of its flowers and sugar 'wonderfully above measure doth comfort the heart'. In the fourteenth century, the blooms of a fringed white pink were dunked in wine to impart a spicy savour – hence the name Sops-in-Wine. Both types prefer rather dry soil and full sun.

Sweet william (*Dianthus barbatus*), a relative of the garden pink, is another old cottage favourite. Gerard wrote, 'These plants are not used either in meat or medicine, but esteemed for their beauty to decke up gardens, the bosomes of the beautiful, garlands and crownes for pleasure', and were used in gardens more to 'please the eye, than either the nose or belly'. During the nineteenth century, sweet william became a Florist's flower, along with its cousin the laced pink, and was particularly favoured by Scottish Florist societies. It is a perennial, but usually treated as a biennial. Sow the seed where it is to flower; also look for self-sown seedlings that can be transplanted.

EASTON
HAMPSHIRE

Sweet peas flowering, chrysanthemums growing strongly, peas laden with shiny green pods behind rows of ferny-leaved carrots, this kitchen garden is spread like a delicious welcoming mat before the home of a retired professional gardener, who began his career at the age of fourteen as one of sixteen gardeners on a wealthy estate. He was the 'garden boy', sweeping up leaves, fetching and carrying, and all the while being shown by the senior gardeners the correct and easiest way to do the numerous tasks that were to become his stock-in-trade. Today he says that gardening 'is not the same job', due to all the machinery, chemical sprays and fertilizers that make gardening so much easier. But for all the wonders of modern science, he reminds us, if plants are not watered correctly, our efforts are wasted.

It is easy to distinguish the garden of a retired professional: it is well ordered, and contains within its boundaries all the elements of the grand gardens he has worked in. There will be an immaculate vegetable garden and a length of herbaceous border, a collection of interesting shrubs, a display of annuals neatly bedded out, a well-stocked greenhouse, frames and a compost heap. These are all features of many gardens, but when tended by a professional they acquire a certain gloss that comes from confidence and pride in skills acquired through years of apprenticeship and experience. 'Come, my spade. There is no ancient gentlemen but gardeners, ditchers, and grave-makers; they hold up Adam's profession.' (*Hamlet*, William Shakespeare).

MONXTON
HAMPSHIRE

The many different types of creeping thyme make weed-smothering groundcover, and during late June to July are covered in minute flowers in shades of lavender blue and pink. They are especially useful for edging paths and drives, where they yield the scent of their leaves when they are crushed underfoot. Garden seats and paths covered in creeping scented plants such as thyme and chamomile were a popular feature of Renaissance pleasure gardens, and at Sissinghurst, Vita Sackville-West created a small thyme lawn made of *Thymus serpyllum*, and '... the sort called coccineus to give the redder patches, and also a little of the white, which varied the pattern'. There are thymes with variegated leaves: 'Golden Variegata', 'Silver Posie'; and others with soft grey leaves: 'Woolly doerfleri'. Thyme does not have to be mowed, but should be dead-headed; this gardener uses a 'strimmer', an efficient way to execute an otherwise back-breaking task.

The junction of the path and circular drive marks one end of a curved bed planted with many low-growing shrubs; there are sink gardens at each end of the bed, holding a wide variety of dwarf perennials. Cushions of the bright blue dwarf bellflower, *Campanula persicifolia*, complement the lavender-hued thyme on the opposite side of the drive, from which paths lead into the other parts of the garden.

Gertrude Jekyll described the perfect setting for water lilies as being one that has 'a near surrounding of wooded rising ground', with the trees 'at such a distance as to shut in the scene and to promote stillness of the water surface', and in order to achieve the best garden picture, advised simplicity in planting and avoidance of the use of too many varieties of water plants in one pond. The rising banks of the bowl-shaped enclosure protect this small woodland garden from disturbing gusts of wind and intrusive noises from outside. The stillness through which one moves, along winding paths among the shrubs and evergreens, conduces restful contemplation of the pond, with its rose-tinted lilies, and goldfish sparkling just below the water's surface.

On entering the woodland garden, with the pond to the right, directly ahead is a tumulus of flowering shrubs, specimen conifers, ferns and hosta and the climbing rose 'Albertine', under which lies buried the massive corpse of a fallen tree. The curiosity piqued, one must go on to see what happens on the other side; thus the rest of the garden is discovered.

It is now July and the Worlds great eye, the Sun is mounted on the highest loft of the Horizon.
. . . and the parched earth would be glad of a draught of Raine to slake her thirst. . . . The
Hedges are full of Berries . . . Pears and Plumbs now ripen apace. . . . Now Courteous Country
man, make hay while the Sun shines, for a day slackt is many pounds lost. . . .'

The Twelve Moneths, M.Stevenson, 1661

Promises made the previous month, of vibrant colours and heady fragrances, are
fulfilled in July: herbaceous borders burst into riotous flower, and the sweet scent
of lavender and lily flavours the warm midsummer breeze.

The art of creating herbaceous flower borders was brought to its highest degree
of sophistication by English gardeners during the late nineteenth to early
twentieth centuries, led by the indomitable Gertrude Jekyll. Her partnership with
the architect Edwin Lutyens resulted in some of the finest country-house gardens
to be created since the eighteenth century, when the landscape movement began to
change the face of English gardens.

In June 1712, Joseph Addison writing in the *Spectator* weighed against the
perfectly formed parterres and formal borders of the Renaissance garden: '. . . the
inhabitants of [China] laugh at the plantations of our Europeans, which are laid
out by the rule and line; because they say, any one may place trees in equal rows
and uniform figures. . . . Our British gardeners . . . instead of humouring nature, love
to deviate from it as much as possible. . . .'

Many agreed with him, and as the gentry vied with each other in their veneration
of Nature, countless miles of box edging were uprooted, parterres grassed over and
flowers banished to the vegetable garden. But they were only substituting one order
for another, for the creation of a 'natural' landscape involved in many cases
uprooting groves of trees, levelling villages and changing the course of rivers.

That flower beds and borders as garden features survived at all is largely thanks
to cottage gardeners. William Cobbett described the making of a flower border in
The English Gardener, first published in 1829. He said that flowers should be

arranged in borders so that 'an infinite variety of them are mingled together, but arranged so that they may blend with one another in colour as well as in stature . . . and so selected as to insure a succession of blossom from the earliest months of the spring until the coming of the frosts.'

A complete understanding of the importance of harmonious blending of floral colour and the manipulation of the myriad subtle tints and shades of leaf and petal was Miss Jekyll's genius. She knew that warm and cool colours should not be allowed to war with each other, but that careful juxtapositions created pleasing visual incidents; that white and silver-leafed plants enriched the intensity of colour groupings; that it was more satisfactory to group together plants with similar flowering times, than to scatter them across the border; and that the perfection of a garden picture was only achieved through a series of carefully constructed compositions. In her book, *Colour Schemes for the Flower Garden*, Miss Jekyll wrote: 'Having got the plants, the great thing is to use them with careful selection and definite intention. . . . It is just in the way it is done that lies the whole difference between commonplace gardening and gardening that may rightly claim to rank as a fine art.'

During July, garden perfumes are as abundant and luxurious as the colours of the flowers that yield them. Many gardeners would agree that 'scents are the souls of flowers', and dedicate their garden schemes to only those plants that have a fine perfume. In so doing they echo the traditions of the ancient gardens of Persia: walled enclosures containing roses and lilies, through which cooling streams ran to fill ponds that provided succour from the arid expanse of the surrounding desert.

European gardens of the fifteenth and sixteenth centuries borrowed this idea, and behind the battlements of castle and fortified manor house lay the 'Ladie's Bower', a pleasure garden planted with scented herbs and flowers: sage, rosemary, bay, mint, roses, lilies and violets. There were shaded arbours of honeysuckle and roses, where 'while the sun was highest one might go all about neath odoriferous and delightsome shade'. Seats were made from thyme and chamomile, and within this garden the chatelaine and her ladies pursued the delights of chivalrous love.

In 1625, Francis Bacon wrote *Of Gardens*, an essay on the proper 'ordering of gardens'. In it he declares that 'nothing is more fit ... than to know, what be the flowers, and plants that do best perfume the air', and holds that the ones most valuable for this purpose are double violets, the musk rose, strawberry leaves 'dying', and sweet briar. Wallflowers should be set under a chamber window; pinks and gillyflowers, lime tree flowers and honeysuckle should also be used. Bean flowers are mentioned but not recommended, as they are flowers of the field – anyone who has driven down a Norfolk country lane in July will be familiar with that seductive perfume – and damask roses and rosemary are two of the plants he deems 'fast of their scent', and so do not contribute to the garden's perfume.

Some flowers with the choicest perfume will not release their scent until the sun is low, and nothing could be sweeter on a still summer evening than to sit in a peaceful arbour planted round with flowers such as the night-scented stock, *Matthiola bicornis*, a dowdy little annual during the day, but come evening a fragrant Jezebel. *Oenothera biennis*, the evening primrose, and *Mirabilis jalapa*, the Marvel of Peru, are old favourites to include in the evening garden.

Pinks, heliotrope, mignonette and lilies, though fragrant during the day, are much freer with their scent at dusk, and the honey scent of the petunia is less cloying in the cool of evening.

A garden of fragrant flowers will be a garden of bees and butterflies. The bees will forage among the blue-flowered herbs and russet-red wallflowers, attracted by the colour, while the butterflies will be drawn by the fragrance of the pale blossoms of pinks and lavender.

At one time a country garden was deemed incomplete if it lacked a row of hives. In 1617, William Lawson, writing in his *Country Houswifes Garden*, stated that 'I will not account her any of my good House-wives, that wanteth either Bees, or skilfulness about them.' Bees were as essential to a garden as the flowers, for honey was necessary for sweetening food and preparing cordials, and was valued as a 'sovereign Medicament both for outward and inward Maladies'. Bees pollinated the orchard and flower garden, and without them fruit would not set nor seed be made for the next year's sowing.

In a Suffolk garden we visited, a special recess was let into the wall, lined with shelves on which stood the hives. Small, decorative windows pierced the side walls so that the bees could have access to the fields without. Traditionally the head of the household would tell the bees of important events affecting the family, as it was believed that the bees would be insulted if they were not the first to be told of any good or bad news, so much a part were they of daily life.

Bee-keepers would rub new hives before use 'with fennel, or other sweet herbs, and sprinkle them also with Honey and Beer . . . or some other sweet liquor'; and the rising swarm would be coaxed into their new home by the sound of 'ringing and tinging' on metal pots and basins, 'for they are so delighted with Musick'.

Contemporary gardens rarely have resident bees, but it is rewarding to grow the plants they love; wallflower, borage, sage, lavender, and winter savory provide a summer-long feast. Gardeners should always try to do their spraying in the evening when bees are not abroad in the garden, for the bees will be poisoned the same as the aphids.

The beauty of the summer garden is celebrated this month with flower festivals held in church and village halls throughout the countryside. Most often the flowers are arranged simply for their beautiful display, but some festivals are given a theme, and the arrangements executed to symbolize aspects of the theme.

There are many legends attached to flowers; all the saints and martyrs of the Christian church have a floral emblem, and this is also true of the holy men and women of Judaism. Some of these associations are found in the excellent *Flowers and Flower Lore*, written in 1884 by the Rev. Hilderic Friend, and may give inspiration when gathering flowers for festivals or domestic decorations.

July 2nd is the festival of the Assumption of the Blessed Virgin, and she is often shown holding a spray of *Lilium candidum*, the Madonna lily. The story is that when the Apostles visited her grave on the third day after her death, they found it empty except for garlands of roses and lilies. As protection against enchantment, Judith wore a garland of lilies when she went to meet Holofernes, and saved the Jewish people from the Assyrians.

The feast of St Anne, who was Mary's mother, also falls in July, and to her is dedicated the wild chamomile, *Matricaria recutita* (syn. *M. camomilla*), because its botanical name can be loosely translated as 'beloved mother' (*mater-cara*).

CORPUSTY
NORFOLK

In 1728, the eclectic architect and landscape designer Batty Langley wrote *New Principles of Gardening*; '... a beautiful rural garden', he decreed, should contain 'green openings like meadows, terraces, fountains, statues, obelisks', because, 'The Pleasure of a Garden depends on the variety of its Parts', creating 'a continued Series of Harmonius Objects, that will present new and delightful Scenes to our View at every Step we take, which regular Gardens are incapable of doing. Nor is there anything more shocking than a stiff regular garden.' Included in the book are a number of plates illustrating how walks should end with 'Views of Ruins, after the old Roman manner', and which helped inspire the fad for follies to decorate the landscaped parks of the late eighteenth century. Langley would have appreciated the garden of this seventeenth-century mill; it is surely one of the most surprising in this book, and perhaps in England!

The vibrant planting in the mill forecourt promises a beautiful garden beyond, but one is still unprepared for the diversity of the planting, to say nothing of the array of gothic 'ruins' and follies, constructed by the owners from architectural bits and pieces, beach rocks and cobbles. In one corner of the garden is a grotto; a meandering path crosses a foot bridge and leads to a castellated turret. These constructions give focus to the different garden areas, but are not simply façades. Walk into the grotto and follow the passage down to a small, iron-grilled embrasure that frames the river and the fields beyond; inside the turret a winding staircase leads to the top, from which another perspective of the garden may be had. These spatial variations give the illusion of a garden that is much larger than its one acre; the miniature masterpiece of design adds immensely to the pleasure derived from the comprehensive collection of plants.

'And the roses – the roses! . . . wreathing the tree trunks and hanging from their branches, climbing up the walls and spreading over them with long garlands falling in cascades – they came alive day by day, hour by hour. Fair fresh leaves, and buds – and buds – tiny at first but swelling and working magic until they burst and uncurled into cups of scent delicately spilling themselves over their brims and filling the garden air.' That particular passage from *The Secret Garden*, by Frances Hodgson Burnett, is recalled by the sight of the voluptuous blooms of a climbing rose, grown from a seedling whose name is unknown. Overburdened with flowers, it cascades from the branches of an old apple tree, in a garden where each turn of the path discloses a new scene to amaze and delight.

No opportunity is missed to create thought-provoking incidents. The niche houses a statue of St Fiacre, who along with St Phocas is one of the patron saints of gardeners. Fiacre was a seventh-century Celtic prince who entered a monastery in the French town of Meaux; to fulfil his vocation, he determined to become a hermit. The abbot allowed Fiacre as much land as he could turn in a day, as well as a hut in the forest. The hermit took up a pointed stick rather than a plough, and so was able to turn a boundary line around a large parcel of land, which became his solitary retreat. Set before his niche are clumps of purple-flowered *Dactylorrhiza elata*, candelabra primulas, hosta and the heart-shaped leaves of ligularia. *Dactylorrhiza* is a member of the orchid family, but quite unlike its exotic relations; it grows and increases from a tuber, and enjoys well-drained but moist soil rich in humus.

In the early hours of the dawn, the heart-shapes and viridian hues of the dew-damp foliage are accentuated. *Hydrangea petiolaris* sends its soft white florets into the branches of an overhanging tree, underplanted with *Ligularia* 'Desdemona' with large purple-green leaves, violets that spread on to the grassy path, and a small rhododendron, 'Temple Bells', that has neat tongue-shaped grey-green leaves. A carved stone urn marks the entrance to this small wooded area, and the charm of the scene demonstrates the importance of the pictorial in achieving a sympathetic garden design.

The kitchen garden is enclosed by the walls of an old grain store; the roof has been removed and the breeze-block walls are gradually being dressed with smooth pebbles and brick arches. The vegetable beds are spread in formal array around a central wheel of herbs before a domed garden pavilion. Peas grow up through discarded iron railings, and the scent of roses and lavender fills the still air. Outside the entrance are set opposing rows of fluted column bases, to mark the beginning of a triumphal approach. This architectural extravaganza – the juxtaposition of humble herb and vegetable with a grandiose garden pavilion – sums up the humour as well as the devotion being lavished on this remarkable garden.

Wells-next-the-sea
NORFOLK

Crouched at the bottom of a railway embankment, the garden of a toll-house blazes with colour: delphiniums and foxgloves, lupins and tall-growing hybrid campanulas were all raised from seed by a gardener who believes in quantity as much as quality. In spring, the embankment is plastered with snowdrops, hyacinths, polyanthus, primroses and daffodils that have steadily increased in number since the original planting of two hundredweight nearly twenty-five years ago. Dozens of cuttings are taken each year, and plants increased by division, for handing out to friends and neighbours; for true to his type, this good gardener believes in sharing his floral wealth. The garden doesn't stop at his gate, either; finding that the abutments of the derelict railway bridge 'offended my eye', he began a planting campaign, and now they are hidden behind a curtain of clematis and cotoneaster: the approach to town is beautified and the gardener's sensibilities appeased.

Marsham
NORFOLK

Thirty-five years ago, the front garden of this eighteenth-century cottage was decked out in box-edged beds of annuals. But ground-elder choked the box, and the prevailing dryness of the soil made watering a grind. So the gardeners sallied forth with packets of perennial seed and cuttings of roses. There are now well over a hundred rose bushes and countless herbs and flowering shrubs chosen to attract every type of wildlife – bees, butterflies, and particularly birds, with the exception of pigeons – to the garden. The loose soil is annually enriched with leaf compost, working naturally into the soil from surrounding trees. Comfrey is another natural fertilizer, and an old tin bath at the back is employed to steep chopped comfrey in water. The liquid makes a good foliar feed and is said to repel aphids. Comfrey can also be used to enrich the compost heap, and is a particularly nourishing mulch.

WIVETON
NORFOLK

Clouds of red valerian, *Centranthus ruber*, create a floral gate where the garden path meets the terrace of a late fifteenth-century house. Gerard had the plant in his Holborn garden in 1597, but wrote that it was then 'not common in England', but because it was much admired for its red colour and its predilection for self-sowing in rocky places, it became much used in the walls and rockeries of cottage gardens.

Sometimes the most pleasing plant groupings are purely haphazard, and arise from flowers that have seeded themselves from another part of the garden. All that is required is a modicum of thinning so the plants can give of their best, and produce a colourful corner such as this. Spears of foxglove, sprays of red valerian and yellow alchemilla, day lilies and tiger lilies, hollyhocks and honeysuckle compose their blooms with roses and clematis to paint a garden picture of uncontrived beauty.

Climbing roses reach the upstairs windowsill, and the open casement frames the view of the flower garden below, so that it is the gardener's pleasure to sit at the window on summer mornings, having breakfast and enjoying the scene before her. During the sixteenth century, plans for domestic gardens placed beds of flowers set in geometric patterns beneath the windows of private chambers, so that the design could be seen, and the perfume of the flowers enjoyed. Called knot gardens, the patterns were established with low hedges of thyme, lavender or other small shrubby herbs, and the sections filled with sweet-smelling flowers.

CERNE ABBAS
DORSET

The sight of lifted bulbs awaiting storage until time to plant them out again concentrates the mind on the beauty of past seasons, as well as on the work in those to come. The poem *Hortulus*, by the tenth-century monk Walafrid Strabo (translated by Rafe Payne), contains some of the most eloquent (and often amusing) descriptions of what it means to create a garden. The hard work and disappointments are balanced by the most gratifying pleasures: 'What is more, those plants that were moved,/ More dead than alive, to the newly dug furrows are now/ Green again; our garden has brought them back/ To life, making them good with abundant growth.'

EAST COKER
SOMERSET

'Love was the Inventer, and is still the Maintainer, of every noble Science. It is chiefly that which hath made my Flowers and Trees to flourish . . . for indeed it is impossible for any man to have any considerable collection of noble Plants to prosper, unless he love them . . . without which they will languish and decay through neglect, and soon cease to do him service.' *Flora: seu De Florum Cultura*, John Rea, 1665. Standing before their cottage, the foundations of which are said to be 600 years old, is a couple who have been gardening together for nearly sixty years. Although time may have slowed their pace, it has not faded the beauty of their garden, or lessened the care with which it is tended. There are quantities of vegetables and fruit, and a single perfect rosebud plucked from the flowerbed to give to a garden lover of a younger generation.

At the turn of the century, this cottage was encircled by a rustic-work veranda, covered by an extension of the thatched roof; a shallow dip in the level of the lawn marks the width of what must have been a beautiful flower-covered shelter.

CERNE ABBAS
DORSET

A neat square of garden at the
end of a terrace row is a
monument to the owner's skill
and industry, for annual
displays such as this require
many hours' work in the
greenhouse, pricking out and
potting on, and just as many in
the border when it is time to
set out the young plants. Also,
much of the seed for the
flowers, and the vegetables in
the kitchen garden behind,
have been saved from the
previous season. Nevertheless,
he feels that his garden is not
especially labour-intensive;
the soil is rich and friable after
years of digging and manuring,
and the beds are raised to
make cultivation and planting
less back-wrenching. But what
is probably most helpful is that
the tasks are now established
in a regular programme – in a
garden particularly,
disorganization is the twin of
procrastination, and both are
thieves of time.

Sunny marigolds, pink-tinted
petunias, lilies and fuchsia and
lavender-blue lobelia are the
mainstay of this bedding. In
such a small garden it was wise
to decide upon one scheme and
then carry it out with gusto;
anything other would have
appeared half-hearted.

During midsummer the annual bedding plants are in full flower. Much has been written deprecating the vogue for bedding out, which reached its apogee with the Victorian gardeners, the colours of the flowers sparring in lurid Technicolor combat. Yet, compatibility is possible: in a basket against a wall, dark lobelia is teamed with ghostly pale fuchsia, the two united in their pendulous habit.

Having decided upon raised beds and built the necessary retaining walls of concrete, the gardener felt their starkness jarred with the vibrancy of the flowers. Never one to let anything go to waste, he began to collect the crockery shards from the plate-smashing stall at church bazaars. With infinite patience, he fixed the pieces to the retaining walls of the flowerbeds in a glossy patchwork. In other gardens, seashells, pebbles, and shards of broken glass have been utilized to the same effect.

ANSTY
DORSET

Gertrude Jekyll wrote that the
difference between inspired
gardening and gardening that
was merely commonplace lay
in the gardener's ability 'to
place every plant or group of
plants with such thoughtful
care and definite intention
that they shall form a part of a
harmonious whole'. While the
painting of beautiful garden
pictures from a palette of
flower colour was her forte,
she recognized the influence of
leaf shape and colour in the
final composition.
'Architectural' plants such as
yucca, *Verbascum vernale*, and
the giant cow parsley,
Heracleum mantegazzianum,
punctuated her border designs;
favourite smaller-leaved
plants included hosta, ferns,
bergenia, and francoa. Here, a
small grouping of plants with
plain, regular-shaped leaves
(ligularia, hemerocallis and
hosta) are played off against
plants with feathered and
spiky foliage.

ANSTY
DORSET

This cottage and garden have
been in the owner's family for
150 years, and the planting of
the front garden has altered
little over the years, proved by
an early watercolour of the
house showing the tree stump
carefully planted then as it is
today. Such continuity is
comforting at a time when so
many old gardens have
disappeared beneath the
developer's bulldozer, or do-it-
yourself crazy paving. It is a
good idea, if acquiring an old
garden when changing house,
to investigate the history of
the place; the discovery of an
old photograph could aid in
the restoration of the garden
to its former glory.

HITCHAM
SUFFOLK

From the road this property appears to be a model cottage garden; in one corner a well-tended vegetable patch, in another a pond, box-edged beds crowded with all the old familiars: roses, honeysuckle, lilies. But a closer look reveals many choice and unusual plants, so it is hardly surprising to discover that the owners are on the staff of the Royal Botanic Gardens at Kew, and that their garden, while designed to be a traditional one, appropriate to the cottage, must also provide a home for rarities collected on plant-hunting trips to Nepal and other far-flung places. One such corner devoted to these treasures is the peat bed, seen nestling under the thatched eaves on a shady side of the house, devoted to a collection of unusual hardy ferns, terrestrial orchids, and blue Tibetan poppies.

The garden was planned around the willow and fruit trees, which were all that remained of the old garden, and the space divided into areas that either provide shade and shelter or else are bright and open, to allow the owners to grow as wide a variety of plant types as possible. Water flows through the property; a pond was created, and of course a kitchen garden.

Astilbes, hosta and alchemilla deck the edge of the small pond, wherein grows the purple-flowered *Iris laevigata* seen against the pale lavender bells of the hosta. This iris has broad-petalled, slightly flat flowers that look as though they have been pressed, but nonetheless have a graceful appearance. It is a close relation of the wonderful *I. kaempferi*, which also appreciates a moist site, but unlike *laevigata* will not tolerate lime. 'Rose Queen' is a hybrid of the two, and is described by Graham Stuart Thomas: 'The broad-petalled flowers with handsome drooping falls are of soft old-rose, very telling in the garden.'

Wheelbarrows full of old lime rubble from a demolished shed were incorporated into the making of a scree garden. Tiny alpine plants that disdain dampness at their bases thrive in the well-drained, alkaline conditions, simulating those of the limestone and granite rubble found at the base of cliffs and mountainsides. Species of saxifrage and sedum, campanula and geranium, send up their sprays of tiny flowers in company with the furry white stars of edelweiss and many other alpine plants.

LOWER UFFORD
SUFFOLK

A garden is not complete without some feature of particular interest or curiosity; it becomes the focal point around which all the other elements of the garden unite. Stately gardens may rely on fountains, topiary or specimen plants of exotic habit, but here the device is a skirt of vibrant Livingstone daisies, also known as mesembryanthemums, billowing about the base of an aged apple tree. The tree no longer provides fruit, but serves as a climbing frame for clematis and home for a clump of *missle*, the local name for mistletoe. Pliny wrote that mistletoe that is sown never sprouts, but must first pass through a bird, where it is 'ripened in the guts'; but this fine clump was 'planted' by the gardener's wife, who, one Christmas, simply pushed the berries into the tree bark. A sprig plucked from an apple tree is traditionally best for bringing luck to a household.

The incandescent skirt of daisies is repeated at the base of a small raised bed, which is planted with a colourful mixture of familiar annuals: pansies, petunias, marigolds, sweet william and alyssum. One foliage plant often encountered in cottage gardens is *Tanacetum densum amanum*, a silvery-grey mop of finely feathered foliage. With the Livingstone daisies, it is well suited to the dry, well-drained conditions of rockeries and walls. At the back of the border a rustic-work arch supports the rambling rose 'Albertine', so popular since its introduction in 1921 that it is unusual to find a garden where it is not growing. Sadly, its flowering season is short, but it compensates by producing masses of flowers in midsummer. Vita Sackville-West described 'Albertine' as 'very strong and free-flowering, a beautiful soft pink that appears to have been dipped in tea'.

LOWER UFFORD
SUFFOLK

The gardener who tends the garden described on the preceding two pages also looks after this herbaceous border, which belongs to the neighbouring cottage; the two are divided by an enclosed garden devoted to early bulbs and other spring-flowering plants. The border is well stocked with many of the popular perennials: groups of azure delphiniums, golden yellow achillea, hollyhocks and Madonna lilies tower over the lupins and the white daisies of *Chrysanthemum maximum*. Maintaining a border to such a high standard requires hard work; plants must be dead-headed as their flowers fade, and every three years this gardener lifts and divides the plants to renew the border. At the same time the beds are dug and manured to maintain their fertility, and to remove any perennial weeds that may have found their way in.

In any cottage garden the hollyhock is sure to be found, planted at the back of flowerbeds or against the cottage wall, each year gaining in height until its uppermost blooms brush the thatched eaves. This native of the Near East has been grown in English gardens for so long that it is intriguing to speculate that it arrived with returning Crusaders: hence perhaps its earlier name of Holy-hock. Cottagers once cultivated it as a pot-herb, and Gerard described the hollyhock's virtues as being similar to, but less efficacious than, those of the wild mallow: 'the leaves of Mallowes are good against the sting of Scorpions, Bees, Wasps, and such like', and a decoction of roots and flowers was recommended as a digestive.

LAVENHAM
SUFFOLK

Lavender cotton, *Santolina chamaecyparissus,* has been grown in cottage gardens for centuries, valued for the pungent aroma of its soft grey foliage and used as a strewing herb, scattered on floors with other aromatic leaves to drive away fleas and other vermin. Dried branches were also hung in wardrobes and put among linen to prevent moth. Early in the seventeenth century, John Parkinson described it as being 'in many places planted in Gardens, to border knots with, for which it will abide to be cut into what forme you thinke best'. To keep the shrub from becoming straggly and untidy, clip it over in the autumn, and then cut hard back every two or three years in the spring. The dwarf form, *nana,* has a neater habit and is best for the small garden.

Of all the flowers, the smell and sight of lavender most immediately conjures visions of English country gardens; banks of the soft grey bushes fogged by a mist of purple flower spikes give off a scent in the midday sun 'piercing the senses' and providing a setting among which other cottage flowers can be placed to perfection. The flowers, gathered and dried when they are half open, can be placed in wardrobes and drawers, or mixed with rose petals to make *pot pourri.* Lavender oil has long been used in perfume and unguents to ease 'cold and benummed parts'; in 1551, William Turner advised a quilted cap filled with lavender flowers to be worn daily as being 'good for all diseases of the head that come of a cold cause' and to 'comfort the braine very well'. The old English lavender, *Lavendula angustifolia,* grows to two feet; *L.* 'Alba' is the same size and has white flowers. Of the dwarf varieties, good for edging, 'Hidcote' has the finest dark purple flowers, 'Munstead' is paler but with a good scent, and 'Nana Rosea' has pink flowers. Clip over after flowering and prune in the spring, taking care to avoid cutting into old wood.

MONKS ELEIGH
SUFFOLK

Until 1907, this pink-washed seventeenth-century cottage was the village inn; today it is a family home, where the owners created a garden intended to be fun for their children. There are dark shady corners and winding paths in and out of the groups of flowering shrubs, and a secret corner nicknamed 'the Lookout', which, because of its sunny aspect, is being planted with fruit trees. Some gardeners are of the opinion that children and gardening do not mix and, certainly, precious plantings are put at greater risk in the presence of footballs and games of hide-and-seek. But the love gardeners feel for their creations can be enhanced by making the garden an extension of the child's universe, thus exposing their children to an appreciation of Nature.

LOWER TASBURGH
NORFOLK

The owner of this garden is a sculptor, and the hand of the artist is evident in the imaginative groupings of unusual plants in a cottage setting. Here lime green *Nicotiana alata* is teamed with rose campion and purple-flowered veronica. Elsewhere in the garden *Acanthus mollis* and *Allium christophii* are paired; both have purple-tinted flowers and strong but contrasting shapes. *Chrysanthemum maximum* grows with white martagon lilies and grey-leaved phlomis sets off the creaminess of the musk rose 'Buff Beauty'. The construction of the herbaceous beds surrounding three sides of the lawn is also of interest; the level of the soil is four or five inches below that of the lawn, which is edged with brick.

MIDDLETON
SUFFOLK

Family heirlooms come in many forms, and these box-edged beds and topiary were originally set out in the 1880s by the present owner's grandfather, who also, in the early 1900s, planted many of the woods in the surrounding area. Originally, the trees were there to provide game cover for nearby estates, but today they have grown into areas of great beauty, enriching the countryside with habitats for native flora and fauna. Both the personal and public legacy are valued and admired by the grandson, who rightly points out that many of England's deciduous forests have been destroyed or are currently under attack, and that not enough is being done to preserve them for future generations, who will be the poorer because of our lack of foresight.

HOLLESLEY
SUFFOLK

Passionflower and honeysuckle wreathe the covered porch, scattering their flowers among those of 'New Dawn' and 'Iceberg' roses. The cottage has been lovingly restored by a couple who have made it their contribution towards preserving the memory of English rural life. The small kitchen is hung with old-fashioned gardening tools, and pictures of cottage gardens festoon the walls. In the garden itself, fruit trees and bushes grow with old-fashioned cottage flowers, and the rock garden is planted with a collection of unusual dwarf evergreens.

MIDDLETON
SUFFOLK

Cottage windows always frame a pot or two of some decorative flowering plant, from simple pelargoniums to tender exotica. The window is the cottager's greenhouse and frame, either an extension of a larger one out in the garden, which allows a closer watch to be kept on difficult treasures, or simply a substitute for the real thing.

The moon daisy, *Chrysanthemum maximum*, began appearing in English gardens in 1816. A native of the Pyrenees, its hardiness, reliability and flower quality soon gave it precedence over the simple marguerite, *C. leucanthemum*, that had been grown in cottage borders since the fifteenth century. The moon daisy is a parent of the large-flowered single hybrids called Shasta daisies, that were developed by the American plantsman Luther Burbank. From his plants have evolved the many cultivars popular today; some are double, and have narrow frilled petals that flutter daintily about the flowers' golden eye. 'H. Seibert' has enormous single frilled flowers; 'Esther Read' and 'Fiona Coghill' are good doubles. They are extremely easy plants to grow given well-drained soil; plant in full sun or partial shade.

The church flower festival had many of its finest blooms from this bed of *Lilium regale* on the day this picture was taken; armfuls were cut from the long rows, growing in well-ordered ranks with broad beans and peas. In the warm sun, the scent was overwhelming and the flowers glistened like porcelain. It was easy to imagine what Ernest Wilson must have experienced when in 1908, in the Chinese province of Hupeh, he first discovered regal lilies growing in naturalized profusion. This lily produces quantities of good seed; as Vita Sackville-West wrote, '*L. regale* will come up as thick as mustard and cress ... think of the economy and of the staggered crop that you can raise, if you sow even one little row of seed every year.' These lilies appreciate enriched soil and good drainage in full sun.

KERSEY
SUFFOLK

A much older denizen of cottage gardens is *Lilium candidum*, the Madonna lily; it acquired this common name late in the nineteenth century, but before that had been known for centuries simply as the white lily. 'The lily is next to the Rose in worthiness and noblenes', wrote the thirteenth-century friar, Bartholomeus Anglicus, and it appears in any number of Renaissance paintings as the emblem of the Virgin Mary.

The earliest European depiction of the lily is in a tenth-century miniature of St Ethelreda, and in the eighth century the Venerable Bede made the lily the symbol of the Virgin Mary's Resurrection. It may well have been introduced to England by the Romans. For all its grand associations and elevated rank, it is a humble flower that grows best in poor limy soil where, buried just below the surface and left undisturbed, it will increase yearly to crown the garden with perfect white flowers, unequalled for their purity and the richness of their perfume.

Late Summer

Now do the Reapers try their Backs and their Arms, and the lusty Youths pitch the sheafs into the Cart, the Furmenty pot welcomes home the Harvest Cart, and the Garland of flowers crowns the Captain of the Reapers; and Oyl and Vinegar dance attendance to the Sallad herbs, while the ripened Fruits dangling down the Boughs, shew the wealth and the beauty of the Earth.'

The Twelve Moneths, M.Stevenson, 1661

This is the month when garden work reaches a hiatus; the spectacular flush of flowers is fading to make way for the softer colours of leaf and berry during autumn. In the kitchen garden and orchard, crops are coming into ripeness, and the gardener can rest a moment before the flurry of harvest-time activity.

Days are getting shorter, and the cooler evening gives rise to a mantle of soft mists over the garden, enhancing the gentler tints.

Kent is called the garden of England primarily because of its hop fields and orchards; travelling along the small country roads, one realizes that the relative smallness of the orchards gives the landscape the intimacy of a private garden, compared to the prairie-like fields of Norfolk and Suffolk.

An orchard was once an integral part of a country garden, for just as the table required fresh vegetables and herbs, so it required sweet fruits and nuts. Yet it was not an orchard for profit alone, but also for pleasure, particularly if the gardener followed the advice given by William Lawson in his treatise *A New Orchard and Garden* (1618). He recommended the placement of mounts, artificially raised hillocks, in corners of the garden, and the creation of walks with seats or banks of chamomile, from which could be viewed 'your Fruit-trees of all sorts loaden with sweet blossoms, and fruit of all tastes . . . your trees standing in comely order, which way so-ever you look'.

There should be borders 'hanging and dropping' with raspberries and currants, and strawberries growing at the base of the trees. Violets and primroses, rosemary and sweet eglantine also had a place in Lawson's orchard, and, if possible, through it should run 'silver streams, you might sit in your Mount, and angle a peckled

Trout, sleighty Eel, or some other dainty Fish'. And to complete the orchard the hum of bees and the song of nightingales should fill the air.

Eleven years later, John Parkinson in his work *Paradisi in Sole, Paradisus Terrestris*, described a more 'workmanlike' orchard, although the frontispiece illustrates Adam and Eve tending the Garden of Eden, which looks much like Lawson's description.

Parkinson's orchard was enclosed by a wall with a broad walk running around the inner perimeter, and had a hedge of roses, gooseberries or currants between the wall and path. The warmest walls of south and southwest aspect had the tenderest and earliest fruits trained against them: apricots, peaches and nectarines; the remaining sides had plums and quinces. Within the orchard itself were plums, cherries and apples, pears and filberts, set so that 'one doe not hinder or spoile another', achieved by planting in diagonal rows, with the trees equidistant from one another.

And today, this is how we find some of the older orchards of Kent planted, although, sad to say, many are being uprooted to be replanted with new fruit varieties, either to make good losses through old age or to conform with Common Market agricultural policy. As a result, many of the old-fashioned varieties have become rarer or have disappeared, and the tastes and colours of autumn harvests become a little duller in the cause of uniformity.

Vegetable gardens have changed too, not least in the varieties of vegetables produced. This is especially noticeable in the vegetables we grow for salad, which if anything are less adventurous than those used in the seventeenth century when John Parkinson described, among other plants, the virtues of lamb's lettuce or corn salad, purslane, chervil, rocket, tansy, burnet, fennel, marigold, clove gilloflowers or pinks (preserved, pickled or sugared), skirrets and parsnips. He mentioned dandelions, but without favour, as being wild and 'used onely of strangers, and of those whose curiositie searcheth out the whole worke of nature to satisfie their desires'.

The kitchen garden was recommended to be on a south-facing slope, the better to catch the warmth of the sun and assist drainage, and surrounded with a high brick wall to contain the warmth. The finer flowers were not meant to be grown in the vegetable precincts, because '. . . your Garden-flowers shall suffer some disgrace, if among them you intermingle Onions, Parsnips . . .', and also because the vegetable garden is constantly altering as crops are lifted and ground manured (a reason for not having the kitchen garden too near the best rooms of the house!).

Nonetheless, the kitchen garden would have been a pretty spot. Imagine the scene as William Lawson describes the herbs necessary in a country housewife's kitchen garden: lavender and roses to border the beds, crocus (grown for saffron), iris (for orris root powder), pinks and marigolds (for the stillroom), violets (for sweets and cordials), poppies, mallow, lilies and 'Daffadowndillies'. And growing against the wall would be the tender fruit trees. What a lovely spot for which to give thanks at Harvest Festival, and to serve as an inspiration to those gardeners who care to bring flowers and a tiny slice of history into the vegetable patch.

The practice of gardening is constantly changing: implements are improved, and scientists cook up new broths to control the garden's pests and diseases, or develop new plants resistant to nasties or simply bigger and better than before. Yet there are aspects of gardening that alter but slightly: for example, the repertoire of garden skills. And this can be seen nowhere more clearly than in old gardening books.

Among these texts we will find all the things we gardeners enjoy most reading about: how to be a good gardener and create a beautiful garden that is a testament to our knowledge and skills; the plants we can grow and how best to grow them; the rarities and exotica that can make a garden more brilliant; and (perhaps best of all) what other gardeners do, and have done, to choke weeds, grow giant marrows, create a showcase or an idyllic setting for private reveries.

Gardeners everywhere can sympathize with the tenth-century monk Walafrid Strabo when, in his endearing poem *Hortulus*, he describes his first encounter with 'this little patch which lies facing east' that was full of nettles. He asks (as we all have done) 'What should I do?', as though the patch were a truculent child of unpleasant aspect that only he could love.

Make a quantum leap, and amble gently through Francis Bacon's garden essay *Of Gardens* (1625), in which he holds that '. . . in the royal ordering of Gardens, there ought to be Gardens for all the months in the year, in which, severally, things of beauty may be then in season'. Leaf through an edition of the herbalist John Parkinson's *Paradisi in Sole, Paradisus Terrestris*, published in 1629, and delight in his descriptions of familiar flowers, *viz.*, 'the great double yellow Spanish bastard Daffodill, or Parkinsons Daffodill. I think none ever had this kinde before my selfe, nor did I my selfe ever see it before the yeare 1618, for it is of mine own raising and flowring first in my Garden.' Gardeners do not change: they are nothing if not proud of their achievements!

Go garden visiting with Sir William Temple, who in 1685 described Moor Park in Hertfordshire as 'the perfectest Figure of a Garden I ever saw, either at Home or Abroad'; and wonder in his description of the perfect seventeenth-century garden with its grottoes, parterres, fountains, and all that declared humanity the master of Nature, for such was the ideal of gardens of that period. Today we visit Hidcote in Gloucestershire, Hestercombe in Somerset and Sissinghurst in Kent for our inspiration, notebooks at the ready. Although their criterion was not to dominate Nature, the designers of these gardens made full use of what she had to offer.

Oddly, in view of the importance attached in the past to harnessing the beauties of Nature, throughout the writings of the eighteenth century's gardeners and garden lovers runs the idea that the garden was but a reflection of their relationship with the Divine Being. But not so odd when one considers their belief that the human race was created in a garden. It was in Eden that Eve was created of Adam's rib: was she the first hybrid?

Witness the venerable James Hervey, who in the mid-eighteenth century published *Meditations and Contemplations*, containing 'Reflections on a Flower

Garden'. In this essay he relates every part of a garden to God, from the first rays of the sun to the fluttering of a butterfly. His reflections, with a bow to modern quandaries, are relevant today: 'In a Grove of Tulips, or a Knot of Pinks, one perceives a Difference in almost every Individual. Scarce any two, are turned, and tinctured, exactly alike. Each allows himself a little *Particularity* in his *Dress*, though all belong to one family: so that they are various, and yet the same.'

William Robinson let loose his wrath upon the florid 'bedding out' of the Victorians, a legacy of the Florists, who, according to William Cobbett writing in 1829, used it as a way of displaying their creations, 'where the whole bed consists of a mass of one sort of flower'. Robinson's banner was hoisted by Miss Jekyll and has not been dropped to this day.

So the theory and practice of gardening has continued to evolve, and with Capability Brown, Humphry Repton, William Robinson, Gertrude Jekyll and others, the quadrille of garden design glides through changing figures.

Today, we are spurred on by the inspired writings of Vita Sackville-West, Margery Fish and Lanning Roper; by the creativity of Russell Page and his *Education of a Gardener* (1962), and by the practical experience of garden creators such as Graham Stuart Thomas and Christopher Lloyd, Sylvia Crowe, and Rosemary Verey. All are English gardeners, and all have something to offer, for garden writing 'travels', with an allowance for local prevailing conditions, just as do the plants we bring into our gardens.

But, as though to wave a remonstrative finger at us, the words of Walafrid Strabo bring us back to basics, and none can better him:

'. . . if you do not
Refuse to harden or dirty your hands in the open air
Or to spread whole baskets of dung on the sun-parched soil –
Then, you may rest assured, your soil will not fail you.
   This I have learnt not only from common opinion
And searching about in old books, but from experience. . . .'

Tyler's Green
EAST SUSSEX

In *The Englishman's Flora*,
Geoffrey Grigson wrote of the
yew that it was a 'protective,
offensively defensive tree, one
of the best to plant by your
house'. In it lived the
household god, and a tree was
most often set on the windward
side, becoming a 'double
protection', for the beneficial
magic began the moment the
small tree was planted, before
it was big enough to shelter
the house from the wind. The
tree also has less benign
connotations: Shakespeare
called it 'double fatal yew', and
so it was, for the berries are
poisonous and yew was the
wood preferred by English
archers for their bows
(although Spanish yew was
superior to native yew for the
purpose). The evergreen yew
was a symbol of resurrection
and afterlife to both pagan and
early Christian; so the Druids
built their shrines near yew
trees, and many churchyards,
built on these same sites,
possess yew trees from which
branches were plucked to
substitute for palm branches
on Palm Sunday.

WILLINGDON
EAST SUSSEX

One of a pair of garden houses designed by Edwin Lutyens and sited above a length of terrace where the border has been planted with many of the flowers, shrubs and climbers used by Gertrude Jekyll, thereby preserving the unity of house and garden in the best traditions of that famous partnership. She wrote that a garden house 'is an outpost where the amenities of the house and its more gentle employments can be enjoyed in a garden atmosphere'. To be successful, it should be linked to the main house through its architectural treatment and to the garden by its period.

CAMBERLEY
SURREY

Narrow raised vegetable beds
separated by a path allow this
gardener to till the soil
without having to walk
between the vegetable rows.
This means that plants can be
grown closer together,
yielding more from less space;
the soil is not compacted and
drainage and aeration are
better, so seed can often be
sown earlier than in flat beds,
and weeds are easier to pull.
Water and fertilizer are
concentrated where they are
needed, rather than being
wasted on paths between rows;
and if a generous amount of
manure is worked into the soil
when the beds are created, and
the garden mulched with
compost, annual spring
digging is eliminated. The
vegetable garden is separated
from the main garden by a
screen of cordon-trained fruit
trees. This is an attractive and
space-saving way to bring fruit
trees into the garden.

The value of the bees to the
gardener is incalculable, for
apart from the honey they
make, as the bees work each
bloom gathering pollen and
nectar to nourish the hive they
also pollinate the plants. There
was a time when no garden
was considered complete
without a hive, and over the
centuries much has been
written on bee-keeping: in the
first century BC, Virgil
recommended planting
'glowing saffron, and fat limes,
and deep-coloured hyacinths'.
It is worth planting drifts of
bee-plants, like these amber
heleniums and steely blue
Echinops ritro, the globe
thistle, for as William Cowper
wrote, 'they pay me for the
honey they get out of it by a
hum, which, though rather
monotonous, is as pleasing to
my ear as the whistling of
my linnets.'

HEATHFIELD
EAST SUSSEX

In 1699, an Italian priest sent a packet of seed collected in Sicily to that 'curious collector and introducer of many rare exoticks', Dr Robert Uvedale of Enfield. From the seeds he grew spindly plants with bicoloured flowers of maroon and lavender blue and extremely pleasing perfume, 'somewhat like Honey and a little tending to the Orange-flower smell' – the original sweet pea. But it was almost 200 years before the flower achieved its well-deserved popularity and became essential to the cottage garden. Seed is usually sown in February under glass and planted out in March for flowers in July, yet Gertrude Jekyll recommended sowing seed in pots under a cold frame in late September to early October. In this way these hardy annuals get a head start, making steady, sturdy growth during winter and producing better flowers earlier. Plant out from early March to April in deeply dug and well-manured soil, and train up rows of canes in the kitchen garden, or through the branches of a brushwood wigwam in the flower border.

'A weed is anything that's growing where it oughtn't,' said the owner of this garden. Fortunately, he approved of the site against the hedge chosen as a self-sown home by a tribe of regal lilies. For fifty-four years he has tended this garden. The cottage was tied to the estate where he had been head gardener, supervising the work of five other gardeners – the culmination of a career that began when he was sixteen. The layout of his garden is much the same as it has always been, the bedding changing with the seasons: wallflowers, tulips and forget-me-nots will be put in after the summer bedding is cleared, to provide the flowers of spring. He saves all his own seed, buying only the occasional packet for a fresh strain, and is nearly self-sufficient for vegetables; what he lacks he gets through barter and exchange, because 'it's the country way'.

FRAMFIELD
EAST SUSSEX

A box-edged herb garden, set below the kitchen window of a half-timbered house nearly 500 years old, was designed by the gardener to be in keeping with the period of the house, and she concentrated on planting those flowers and herbs appropriate to such a garden and which would feed her bees. So successful was she that the garden might be a model for the first garden-skill book specifically for women, which was written in 1617 by William Lawson, and called *The Country Houswifes Garden*. In it he sets out patterns for knots, and lists of herbs and flowers to make 'comely borders' and pretty beds in what was essentially a practical garden. But his sternest words are reserved for the section dealing with the husbandry of bees: 'I will not account her any of my good House-wives, that wanteth either Bees, or skilfulness about them.'

NORTHBOURNE
KENT

'One has the illusion of being an artist painting a picture', wrote Vita Sackville-West of the manipulation of flower colour in the creation of a garden, and although the simile may seem hackneyed, it is the most appropriate, one realizes, when visiting a garden originally planted nearly sixty years ago by a man who was also a skilled watercolourist. Today the garden is cared for by his son, working within the colour plan devised by his father, but altering the plants to maintain the vitality of the garden.

The garden is built on the site of an Elizabethan manor, and consists of a main terrace garden approached through several small garden rooms, in the first of which borders and a tub of geranium and fuchsia bedazzle the eye with tints of red.

In the soft light of a late summer evening, the second walled enclosure contains a quiet harmony of powdery silver foliage and velvet textures. What flower colour there is is as delicate and fleeting as the light. The shelter of the warm brick walls has allowed *Hydrangea sargentiana* to grow into a fine shrub; it is an underappreciated member of the genus, valuable for its bristly textured stems clothed with great green velour leaves under dishes of pale pink florets.

The transition between these first two rooms, the contrast of much with little colour, is stimulating; and of the two, the grey garden seems cooler and more tranquil. The lack of true colour concentrates the attention on the texture of the plants used in a grey garden: artemisia, sage, santolina, and thyme among others.

Leaving behind the stillness of the grey garden, one enters the main garden: three broad terraces rising up on three sides around a central pond. The walls of the terraces are Elizabethan; gardens of that period often had terraces as well as mounts, from which the garden picture of knots and other floral conceits could be more effectively viewed. But today each terrace is planted to make the most of complementary associations; the beds at ground level are of pale-coloured flowers, the first terrace beds are predominantly purple and yellow, and those of the second and third terrace are mainly blue and orange. Sheets of blue-flowered rosemary drape the first wall behind the pale flowers, and lavender tumbles over the remaining two walls. In this warm-toned section of the second terrace, daisy-flowered rudbeckia mingles with nicotiana and bronze fennel.

The large kitchen garden was also planted with an eye to creating effect with massed colour and texture; for example, the entrance path across the width of the garden was edged with clouds of nicotiana, and earlier in the year the lengthwise path would have been nearly obstructed by peonies. Many vegetables have decorative value as well as culinary merit, and can be used to beautify the garden and the home: globe artichokes, allowed to flower, had been gathered for arrangement with flowers from the main garden.

Joseph Addison, writing in the *Spectator* in 1712, declared, 'I have always thought a kitchen garden a more pleasant sight than the finest orangery, or artificial greenhouse. I love to see everything in its perfection: and am more pleased to survey my rows of coleworts and cabbages, with a thousand nameless pot-herbs . . . than to see the tender plants of foreign countries.' Most would agree that a sensation of comfort and contentment is aroused by the sight of a well-tended kitchen garden, row upon row of nourishing vegetables and fragrant herbs composed in a variety of leaf colour and form.

137

Broad, heart-shaped pumpkin leaves of clear green make a bold contrast with a froth of scarlet-flowered geranium. Throughout this garden, one is constantly reminded of another beautiful garden created by an artist: that of the Impressionist master Claude Monet at his home in Giverny. There, too, the concern was with the broad effects created by associations of clear colour and the textures of leaf and flower.

OTHAM
KENT

Fuchsias are among the best plants for flower colour during late summer; compared to the brash dahlias and chrysanthemums that are about, the fuchsia is a paragon of daintiness and delicacy, in both colour and form. There are many cultivars to choose among, some with skirts unbelievably double, others like furled umbrellas, in shades of rose, purple-pink and white. These are most effective grown in containers and set out in the garden, but there are types that are extremely useful in the border: *Fuchsia magellanica* 'Aurea' has golden-yellow leaves veined red, and bears red flowers; *F. m. gracilis* 'Versicolor' has soft grey-green leaves that are tinged pink when young and variegated creamy white as they mature, and is a particularly nice addition to a grey garden. 'Riccartonii' is the old cottage-garden favourite, and extremely hardy.

LYMINGE
KENT

Sculptured ornaments have long had a place in the garden; fountains, statuary and obelisks have all been popular at one time or another. But sundials have a special fascination, due no doubt to their mixture of science and sentiment, for no good sundial is without a motto, most often reminding us of the fleeting nature of time and our mortality: *Volat tempus*, Time flies; *Ut hora, sit vita*, Life is as an hour. Unaware of time's inexorable flight, the gardener's grandchildren annually hunt their Easter eggs in the box parterre surrounding the sundial.

WEST MALLING
KENT

A neat geometry of clipped box and raked sand recalls the fashion for parterres from an earlier period: in 1724, Phillip Miller wrote in his *Gardener's Dictionary*, 'In a fine Garden, the first thing that should present itself to the sight, is a parterre, which should be next to the House, whether in the front or on the sides, as well upon account of the Opening it affords to the House, as for the Beauty with which it constantly entertains the sight from all the windows on that side of the House.' Certainly, such a treatment of a small front garden is more interesting and impressive than a patch of dull lawn.

OTHAM
KENT

Joseph Addison stated that the only order he imposed on his garden was to 'range in the same quarter the products of the same season, that they may make their appearance together, and compose a picture of the greatest variety'. This is precisely what the owners of this new garden have done. Created on the site of a tarmac playground, opposite borders follow each other through summer, distinguished by the colours of the flowers they contain: one devoted to shades of blue, pink and lavender, of which this is a small section, the other to orange, yellow and grey.

In August, the gold and grey border is at its best with rudbeckia, inula (with attractive fluffy seedheads), Shasta daisies, alchemilla and achillea in full flower. Clumps of grey-leaved senecio and lamb's ears moderate the brightness. When creating such a border it is not enough to use flowers simply within one monochromatic scale; the result would be flat and uninteresting. Contrasts and complements must be used to emphasize the tonal range, creating high and low 'colour pitches' along the border.

Crinum × powellii is a deliciously fragrant member of the amaryllis family. The flowers flare out from the top of stout stems up to four feet tall, and make quite a spectacular show from late summer until the end of autumn. The leaves are rather less spectacular, and can be downright untidy. Crinum grow from huge bulbs; they prefer well-dug, moisture-retentive soil and an annual manure mulch. The species are native to southern Africa, and although hardy in moderately cool climates, will benefit from being planted next to a warm sunny wall.

WITTERSHAM
KENT

With four small children to care for, the owner of this garden felt she needed a hobby to provide another interest, but one that she could pursue at home. Gardening provided the answer. Drawing on her husband's experience as a professional gardener and a neighbour's advice, in the space of five years she has progressed from keen novice to cup winner in the village flower show. Betraying a love of big showy flowers, particularly dahlias, the garden brims over with gladioli, sweet peas, daisies, and love-in-the-mist raised from seed and cuttings – any leftovers are sold from the box perched on the hedge. Her husband's vegetables and the stone sinks at the back for the children to plant add to the garden's variety.

WITTERSHAM
KENT

For some owners, their
gardens are like family
photograph albums, each plant
a reminder of people, places or
occasions. Such is the garden
of this 500-year-old house, the
family's home for twenty-five
years. Sadly, the family were
moving at the end of the
summer, leaving behind the
pair of trees bought by their
daughter with her first
earnings. But the pretty border
stocked with shrubs and
flowers will provide cuttings,
so that old associations can be
renewed in a new garden.

WITTERSHAM
KENT

A wide variety of dwarf
perennials and alpine plants
are spread like a Persian
carpet before a neat weather-
boarded cottage in a variation
on the knot-garden theme.
This is a particularly effective
way to make use of the
carpeting potential of these
low-growing plants, many of
which form colourful
hummocks to soften the edges
of brick-paved paths.

The village church provides a splendid backdrop for the herbaceous border in a garden that cleverly combines a diversity of planting treatments. To get the most from a small garden, a gardener must be resourceful; and in this garden, a retired tea-planter has adapted some of the horticultural techniques of an Indian tea plantation, such as pruning and training a tree to make an area of shade in an otherwise sunny border.

Bright yellow potentilla and violas, lavender-pink hosta flowers and hydrangea, purple hebe and pansy marry in a section of the border that will soon be altered when the chrysanthemums and sedum begin their autumn flowering. Each season has its own colour personality: spring tints are shy; summer is extrovert; and autumn mellow. A garden will feel more comfortable if this is exploited in the planting.

Another corner of the garden serves as the shrubbery, where leaf colour and texture is the main concern; grey-green phlomis, cistus and lavender are blended with golden-green whipcord hebe and perfectly clipped topiary of golden variegated box. At the back, a variegated ivy winds through the branches of an evergreen in company with the beautiful *Clematis florida bicolor* (*syn.* 'Sieboldii'). Its flowers resemble those of the passionflower, with plum-purple stamens surrounded by creamy-white sepals.

MERSHAM
KENT

Actinidia chinensis is probably more familiar as the source of a culinary delicacy than as a decorative climber; its fruit is commonly called the Kiwi, or Chinese gooseberry. But its enormous broad velvety leaves make it worthy of a place in the garden scheme. The flowers are also curiously beautiful, pale apricot in colour, rather like fleshy dog roses; to have fruit you must plant a male and female. Its relative, *A. kolomikta*, is more familiar, with the tips of its leaves faded white and touched with pink.

OTHAM
KENT

An abundance of favourite cottage-garden plants tumble along the borders edging the path to a half-timbered cottage, located in what is one of the oldest settlements in southern England. Many of the plants are left to seed themselves, joining in a cheerful welcome with a variety of shrubs and herbs. Elsewhere there is a paved seating area and flower borders edging the gravel drive, and a water garden being made within the walls of an ancient malt house. In all these places the initial planting is directed by the gardener, but then it is left to the plants to disperse themselves, with a modicum of outside interference.

It is often advisable not to be in too much of a hurry to tidy a border after the flowers have faded; not only can self-sown seedlings be welcome, but the seedheads that form create another garden picture, one of subtle tints and curious shapes. In late summer shades of red and gold predominate, and in this border the russet seed discs of honesty harmonize with pink phlox and chrysanthemum; grey-green glaucous leaves of sedum and yellow bracts of euphorbia echo the colour of inula and black-eyed rudbeckia.

HOLLINGBOURNE
KENT

While it is true that a house and its garden should be treated as one unit, one half of the partnership will always take precedence. Here the garden seems to have cast its sister in the supporting role, and the early fifteenth-century yeoman's hall, buffeted by hydrangeas and cotoneaster, and heavily mantled in ampelopsis, yields a preview of the garden beyond the gate.

Described by its creator as 'horticulturally indigestible', this garden beguiles the senses with the sweet perfumes of herbs and old-fashioned roses, and with beautiful contrasts of leaf and flower. An indication of earlier glories is given in the seedheads, which are allowed to dry on the plants. These are later gathered for sowing or brought into the house for decoration. Paths wind through banks of herbs and old roses leading to quiet arbours, where thoughts turn to the love and humour that is so much a part of this and many other cottage gardens.

Photographing plants, both individually and in a garden setting, is not all that different from photographing people. The object, to convey a sense of the garden's atmosphere, and to show the plants sympathetically, requires working with the available light and conditions as found in each garden. All the photographs in this book were taken on a Pentax LX, which is a 35 mm single lens reflex camera, because the 35 mm system provides the flexibility necessary when working outdoors. It also allowed me to work quickly and spontaneously, which was particularly important as I was nearly always photographing at the extremities of the day when the light is changing minute by minute.

Flowers, like people, photograph much better out of harsh, direct sunlight. In a garden, the bright light of a sunny day, reflecting off myriad surfaces, burns out the rich colours of flower and foliage, and subtle shapes are lost. The majority of the photographs were taken just after dawn or in the early evening as the sun was setting, though some were taken when the day was lightly overcast or cloud cover diffused the light, creating interesting effects. In midsummer, it is light by five o'clock and at eight too bright to work; in the evening work would start between six and seven and carry on until nine. So the remainder of the day was spent researching the gardens and assessing at which end of the day to photograph them.

To get the best picture quality in these varying light conditions I used Kodachrome 25 or 65 ASA, as the images on the faster E6 Process films are more likely to break up and be less distinct in printing, resulting in poorer-quality reproduction.

When working with light at such low intensities, the depth of focus can be a problem. In many of the shots where the main point of interest is in the foreground and a more distant part of the garden is also included, I endeavoured to have both planes of the photograph in focus by stopping down to a small aperture and using a long exposure. I had to use a tripod for most of the shots to keep the camera steady, but this didn't help on the occasions when the wind was blowing. There is no way of arresting the movement of plants in a breeze, and one has to be ready for the instant when the wind drops. Patience can be a great asset to a photographer working in a garden.

The majority of the photographs were taken on a 28mm lens, except in the case of close-ups (flower portraits), when I used a 90 mm Macro lens. The 28 mm seems to give enough sense of space in a garden photograph, but must be used carefully as it can distort perspective, or leave a vast expanse of empty lawn filling half the frame. One must be sure that vertical lines are straight, and keep an eye on the amount of foreground included; it helps to shoot from a low position.

Just as the actual physical composition of a garden is improved if there is some central element or theme to unite the various parts, a photograph of a garden will be more effective if there is one thing in it upon which the observer's eye can focus. It can be the corner of a building or wall, or a garden ornament and needn't be in the centre of the composition. Photographing gardens with the house as a backdrop gives scale and sense of place to the picture, but the house must be kept in the background and not dominate the subject of the picture. At the same time, the architectural element included should have some merit of its own.

Yet in spite of the various problems and the limitations they imposed, I found while working on this book that there were times when just being in these exquisite places at dawn or dusk, with the light filtering through roses and apple tree branches, in the stillness particular to those times of day, the photography just took care of itself.

Clay Perry

Bibliography

Bunyard, E.A. *Old Garden Roses*, Country Life, 1934

Coats, Alice M. *Flowers and Their Histories*, A. & C. Black, 1968
Cobbett, William *Cottage Economy*, 1822; Oxford University Press, 1979
Cobbett, William *The English Gardener*, 1829; Oxford University Press, 1980

Earle, Mrs C.W. *Pot Pourri from a Surrey Garden*, Smith-Elder, 1897; as *Mrs Earle's Pot Pourri*, BBC, 1982
Evelyn, John *Kalendarum Hortense*, 1667

Fish, Margery *A Flower for Every Day*, Faber, 1981
Friend, Rev. Hilderic *Flowers and Flower Lore*, 2 Vols, 1884

Grigson, Geoffrey *The Englishman's Flora*, Phoenix House, 1955; Granada, 1975

Hibberd, Shirley *Familiar Garden Flowers*, Cassell, Petter, Galpin, 1897
Hole, S. Reynolds *A Book About Roses*, Arnold, 1902
Hyll, Thomas *The Profitable Arte of Gardening*, 1568

James, John *The Theory and Practice of Gardening*, 1712
Jekyll, Gertrude *Annuals and Biennials*, Country Life, 1916
Jekyll, Gertrude *Colour Schemes for the Flower Garden*, Country Life, 1936; Antique Collectors' Club, 1982
Jekyll, Gertrude *Roses for English Gardens*, Country Life, 1902; U.S.A. as *Roses*, Ayer, 1983
Jekyll, Gertrude *Wall and Water Gardens*, Country Life, 1901; as *Wall, Water and Woodland Gardens*, Antique Collectors' Club, 1981

Jekyll, Gertrude *Wood and Garden*, Longmans, 1899; Antique Collectors' Club, 1981; U.S.A. Ayer, 1981
Jekyll, Gertrude and Weaver, Lawrence *Gardens for Small Country Houses*, Country Life, 1912

Langley, Batty *New Principles of Gardening*, 1728
Lawson, William *Country Houswifes Garden*, 1617
Lawson, William *A New Orchard and Garden*, 1618

McClean, Teresa *Medieval English Gardens*, Collins, 1981
Miller, Phillip *The Gardeners Kalendar*, 1775 (16th edition)

Page, Russell *The Education of a Gardener*, Collins, 1962
Parkinson, John *Paradisi in Sole, Paradisus Terrestris*, 1629; Methuen, 1902
Paul, William *The Rose Garden*, 1848; Heyden, 1978

Robinson, William *The English Flower Garden*, John Murray, 1903 (14th edition)
Rohde, Eleanour Sinclair *The Old World Pleasaunce*, Jenkins, 1925

Sackville-West, Vita *In Your Garden*, Michael Joseph, 1951
Sackville-West, Vita *Vita Sackville-West's Garden Book*, Michael Joseph, 1979
Strabo, Walafrid *Hortulus*, translated by Rafe Payne, U.S.A. Hunt Botanical Library, 1966
Strong, Roy *The Renaissance Garden in England*, Thames & Hudson, 1979

Thomas, Graham Stuart *Old Shrub Roses*, Dent, 1980
Thomas, Graham Stuart *Perennial Garden Plants*, Dent, 1982

Index